T0209929

Naked in the Middle of a Tornado

The True Story of One Family's
Unbelievable Fight Against It All!

Robert Patrick Herman

WESTBOW
PRESS®
A DIVISION OF THOMAS NELSON
& ZONDERVAN

Scripture taken from the New King James Version®. Copyright © 1982 by Thomas Nelson. Used by permission. All rights reserved.

WestBow Press books may be ordered through booksellers or by contacting:

WestBow Press
A Division of Thomas Nelson & Zondervan
1663 Liberty Drive
Bloomington, IN 47403
www.westbowpress.com
1 (866) 928-1240

ISBN: 978-1-9736-3910-7 (sc)
ISBN: 978-1-9736-3912-1 (hc)
ISBN: 978-1-9736-3911-4 (e)

Library of Congress Control Number: 2018911056

Print information available on the last page.

WestBow Press rev. date: 10/08/2018

This book is dedicated to
my selfless kidney donor,

Linda, my wife,
and Kaley and Journey Herman,
our daughters,
who inspire me everyday to be better no matter what,

to my mom,
Patricia A. Herman,
and my dad,
Robert (Bob) Herman
who "Never Gave In",

to every doctor who had a
positive impact on me, and my perplexing health,
especially

Dr. William Bennett, Legacy, Portland, OR
Dr. Julie Tank, Legacy, Portland, OR
and

Dr. Paul Andrews, Mayo, Scottsdale, AZ
Dr. Ray Heilman, Mayo, Scottsdale, AZ
Dr. Dan Johnson, Mayo, Scottsdale, AZ

Contents

Foreword

"When the going gets tough the tough get going." Knute Rockne (1888-1931)

It has been my pleasure to care for and get to know the Herman family in the course of their tortuous journey with autosomal dominant polycystic kidney disease (ADPKD). Like all patients and their families who go through this experience the disease affects everyone, not just those diagnosed with the disease. In his book, "Naked in the Middle of a Tornado", Rob Herman describes the multi-generational history of his family dealing with this disease with all its physical and emotional toll on multiple members of his family. The word that best describes this journey is courage. For my entire medical career, I have often marveled at the courage individuals with chronic kidney diseases must display to be able to get through the process. In 2018, the journey is even more difficult because of our fragmented health care delivery systems, the difficulty in accessing specialty care, and of course the great emotional and financial toll that inevitably follows.

Rob Herman's book details the highs and lows of his own personal journey and will be an inspiration and a tribute to his family and multiple friends. Much of the credit for his own and his wife, Linda's courage and ability to adapt are related to their religious faith. The comfort that they get from that faith shines through in the book.

Much of the medical progress in ADPKD originated in Kansas City, Missouri, with the formation of the PKD Foundation by Mr. Joseph Bruening. I remember fondly sitting in a hotel room in the early 1980s with Mr. Bruening, Dr. Jared Grantham, who recently passed away, and other luminaries in the field (of which there were few at the time). The Foundation was part of a strategy which has become successful in stimulating PKD research and PKD awareness. There was virtually no research in PKD prior to that time. Now there are drugs approved to slow the progression of PKD. Dr. Grantham was an inspiration to me and all of those who knew him as the driving force, the intellectual spark for much of the research that has led to our current understanding of the disease. Yet we are still only part way through the journey to achieve a cure or even prevent ADPKD. This is crucial for future generations.

Rob and Linda Herman have been an inspiration to me and many others with whom they interact. I admire their courage, faith and dedication to their family and the cause of advancing care for individuals with PKD. I know you will find this book an interesting and revealing insight into what the everyday life of a PKD patient is like. This will hopefully lead you to understand more fully your own journey and experience with PKD and to hopefully realize that everyone including your family, friends, and relatives, as well as your doctors are all in this together, hoping to find ways of mitigating this terrible disease.

William M. Bennett, MD
May 1, 2018

The historic glory of America lies in the fact that it is the one nation that was founded like a church. That is, it was founded on a faith that was not merely summed up after it had existed; it was defined before it existed.

~ G. K. Chesterton ~

Double Agent Escapes To America

If I'm going to share with you the story of four generations, and their losing struggle against an insidious disease, that you may never heard of, then we first have to go back to in time...

This story begins where WWI ends - in 1918. My family's heritage hails from Czechoslovakia (or the Czech Republic, as it's known today), which became its own sovereign state in 1918 after fighting out from under Austrian rule during WWI. The Czechoslovakia Legion – an all volunteer army, which fought in WWI, then became involved in Russia's Civil War after Czech Legion prisoners were taken into Russia. The prisoners revolted and fought alongside the Allies = America, British, and French - in fighting the Bolsheviks in Russia. Simply put: the Bolsheviks wanted communism while other Russian groups, along with the Allies, were willing to die for freedom.

Demeter Herman was a soldier in that Czech Legion. He was young - only 18 - tough, and smart. He also spoke <u>five</u> languages.

Oh, and... he was also... a <u>double</u> agent!

Word had reached Demeter that the Bolshevik Russians discovered he was a double agent. He was going to be "arrested", which meant tortured first, then killed. Why is all this important? Because Demeter was... my grandfather... my dad's dad.

So in the middle of the night Demeter took his wife, Mary Herman, and what they could, including forged papers, to try to escape the country. Poland was not far away and they made it to the border. After some time in line, Demeter and Mary nervously stepped up to present their identification papers to the guard. The border guard looked at the documents, then Demeter, then the documents, repeatedly. The guard grew suspicious of Demeter's papers and told him "to wait right there." The guard left to go check with his superiors.

A disturbance in another lane would save double agent Demeter's life - and the *entire* Herman history. It seemed a lady was causing some concern and the guard did not speak the woman's language. Demeter, who remember spoke five languages, knew what she was saying and intervened, helping rectify the situation. The guard was so grateful of his help that he asked Demeter and Mary how he could help them. They informed the guard they were in a hurry and needed to pass through. He passed him through into Poland. And just in time as the other guard was coming back with soldiers to "arrest" them. For the rest of his life, Demeter Herman - my grandfather - would constantly worry about being caught, even while living in America.

Demeter and Mary (we called her "Baba", which is grandmother in Czechoslovakia) always knew America was "the Land of Freedom", and the chance for a better life for their future family. So they did whatever they had to do to save up enough money for the expensive, and long, trip to America. They managed to get from Poland to France via train - a trip that took "at least a few weeks" back then. Once in France, they made their way onto a ship for a trip which would take over seven days. The RMS Aquitania was headed for America. It was 1921.

They made it to America – the Statue of Liberty and Ellis Island - on June 10th. Demeter and Mary were both just twenty years old and they had very little to their names. But the couple had faith, big dreams, and a *"never give in"* determination.

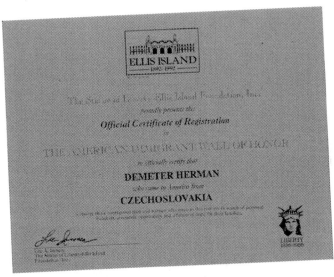

Back in the early 1900s getting through Ellis Island and into America was not as easy as it is today. The process was long, often lasting many days. Demeter and Mary were there for 3

long days. Baba was strip-searched for lice and other ailments. It was a humiliating experience, especially for a modest woman, that left her crying.

To learn if your relatives came through Ellis Island go to: www.libertyellisfoundation.org

The Herman's settled into the steel mill town of Johnstown, PA, the town famous for The Great Flood of 1889, and the "Second Great Flood" in 1977. They would have nine more children, for a total of ten (Their first child, John, died very young in Europe). They would name their fifth baby John also, and *he* would also die as a young boy. My dad, Robert John Herman, born in 1938, is the eighth child.

These Herman's have cancer in there DNA, but not Polycystic Kidney Disease (PKD); the Bako's (Mom's side) carry the PKD gene.

On my Mom's side, great Grandfather John Kula and great Grandmother Sophie Kula were *also* from Czechoslovakia, and knew America was "the Land of Freedom". They arrived in America on March 2, 1921. They also went through Ellis Island, just three months earlier than the Herman's did. They also settled into Johnstown, PA and had a child named Anna Kula, who would become Anna Bako, my mom's mom. Guardian angels hard at work!

John Bako Sr., my great grandfather, (had PKD), and Anna Straka – my great grandmother, had seven children. After John and Anna died in a car accident, John <u>Jr.</u> - the oldest child – was forced to raise his six siblings. This would be the beginning of *kids,* having to raise *kids,* in our family.

John Bako Jr. married Ann Kula (now Bako), and they had four kids; my mom - Patricia Ann (born in 1939) was the oldest by eight years. My grandfather, John Jr., (who I also never met) was an alcoholic, and had Polycystic Kidney Disease.

Dialysis was *very* primitive back then, and one uncle even refused dialysis, and died from PKD. The first dialysis machine was invented in the early 1940's, but the first successful dialysis wasn't until 1945. (More on dialysis later.)

Unfortunately, I do not know much about how my mom grew up; she rarely talked about her childhood. Why would she? From what little I do know, her childhood was very painful. I remember my dad telling an occasional story of how abusive Mom's dad was when he drank. He would regularly come home drunk after work. He would begin by screaming and yelling at his wife, Baba. After she hid or left, he would continue his belittling tirades on his oldest daughter – my mom, Pat.

Mom was abused by not only her alcoholic father, but also by her not-so-nice mother. It was a trickle down effect: father abuses wife (and daughter), and then wife/mom abuses oldest daughter. Oldest daughter (my mom) was in charge of taking care of the house, and her three much younger siblings. If Baba Anna didn't like the way something was done, or not done, my mom got it. "It" was a paddle or stick, but punishments always included having to *kneel on rosary beads*, in a corner, for long periods of time. I believe this is reason why my mom developed such a tough demeanor.

My grandfather, John Jr. would die of kidney failure due to PKD when he was only 45 year old. Baba Anna would outlive her own daughter, my mom. Do you think she attended her child's funeral?

Dad grew up in a *very* small home – 2 bedrooms, 1 toilet - NO shower – on B Street in Johnstown. Remember, they had eight kids – ten people - in that small house. To say they were poor is, of course, an understatement, yet they never took a dime of assistance. One bedroom was turned into two with a curtain. 3 boys slept on a standard sized twin bed. The toilet was in the damp basement, and they cleaned up in the kitchen sink. Baths were every Saturday in a wash tub in that cold, poorly lit basement. I remember that old basement from visiting as a child; I think I went down there once, it was so scary.

During his senior year in high school, my dad was the stage manager for the theatre/plays. My mom had a part in a play. Dad was supposed to make a phone ring which Mom would answer. Well, Dad couldn't get the phone to ring - until after she picked it up – causing some embarrassment to Mom, but the audience loved it, laughing hysterically. Mom pulled Dad aside after the play to chew him out. The next thing they knew, they started dating. I'm not sure who charmed who there.

Dad enlisted in the Air Force after high school for 3 years overseas. It was November 26 - Thanksgiving, 1959, when Mom and Dad got married in Pennsylvania, with a short honeymoon in New York City. My sister, Laura, was born a year later. It was a very difficult delivery due to major hemorrhaging, suspectedly from her PKD. She would need to be revived for - the first of several times - during her life.

Mom worked at General Electric. After his military service, Dad enrolled and graduated from a 21 month course as an electronic technician. He was then hired by GE, but work was always iffy. My sister, Janice, was born 1962.

Mom had friends in Los Angeles, CA, so they moved across the country for more stable work. She knew Dad's dream job was working for IBM - the company of all companies back then! So she encouraged and pushed him to interview. It took 4 days and lots of testing, but he was hired at age 27 for $675 a month. Dad's career was set.

I am convinced that, except in a few extraordinary cases, one form or another of an unhappy childhood is essential to the formation of exceptional gifts.

~ Thornton Wilder ~

During My Beginnings

South Gate and Lynwood are adjoining cities located in the (dead) center of Los Angeles, CA. Both cities are infamous for the 1965 Watts riots. I, Robert Patrick Herman, named after my mom and dad, was born in Lynwood, CA on August 13th, 1965 - that's *FRIDAY,* the 13th during that *riot*! Mom always told me we could see the towns burning from our hospital room window. Throughout our stay, the injured and dying were brought in. (I used to tell people it was a party for me that got out of hand!)

Eventually the rioting would calm but the South Gate house we rented for $100 a month would never again feel safe. Dad's career at IBM fixing and installing computers was off to a good start. Personal laptops and cell phones did not exist back then. I'm talking huge, mega computers that often needed a crane to be lifted into place.

My parents soon made the very wise decision to move my sisters Laura (5 yrs older), and Janice (3 yrs older), and myself, out of Los Angeles. (Thank you!) We moved about 30 miles east to the very small, newly established, town of Walnut, CA: few streets, no grocery stores, lots of beautiful (brown) rolling hills, a few creeks, and some old barns.

Our small home would soon welcome its sixth member of the Herman clan, my brother Daniel (2 yrs younger). Dad still worked in L.A. so his commute went from a few minutes to a few hours each way! That's one commute sacrifice I wouldn't appreciate until I had to do it for my career.

A few things worth noting during my initial, *critical*, early years of life:

I was dropped on *my head* by my sister Laura (age 6) as she was trying to take me out of my crib when I was 1 1/2 years old; it gave me a concussion. (And probably a lot of other problems.)

When I was 2 1/2 years old, my dad had to take me to the hospital because I was having severe breathing problems. I was diagnosed with bronchitis and the doctors said I may have died if I wasn't taken to the Emergency Room.*

That was the crazy beginning to what would end up being a very challenging, medically complicated, yet incredibly blessed life.

In 1970, I was 5 and gas was thirty cents a gallon. I attended kindergarten at Vejar (vA-har) Elementary which was just a block away from our home. One day while in school I was sucking on a piece of hard candy and it got stuck in my throat. I was choking - but too embarrassed to say anything. I got up from my seat and got a drink from the water fountain in our class, trying to get it down my throat. I know, not smart! I went back to my seat. "What should I do?", I thought. I was panicking, and crying, but too stubborn to hit someone and get their attention.

Then, suddenly, I don't know how or why, the piece dislodged back into my mouth. The incident was incredibly scary.* It was the first of many of what I perceive as brushes with my own mortality.

Rob was Mr. America in the play, "It's a Small World".

11

Dinner in the Herman household was always at 5:00pm sharp. Grace was always said in unison: *"Bless us oh Lord, and these thy gifts for which we are about to receive from thy bounty through Christ, our Lord. Amen"* When we were finished eating EVERYTHING on our plate we asked, "May I be excused?" We then took our plate to the kitchen and helped clean up. We were all taught to pitch in and help as a team, a family.

I was 6 years old in 1st grade. I attended St. Martha's Catholic School, and yes, the nuns were tough - but fair. At this school our playground was the church parking lot - all black-top - no grass. My friends and I always played football - touch, of course. One day while we were playing touch football the school bully decided he was going to jump in - literally. He proceeded to *jump* on me, slamming me into the asphalt, as I was running for what I thought was going to be a touchdown. I slowly got up, screaming and crying.

And then - the recess bell rang.

Now in Catholic school when the recess bell rings everyone has to stop what they are doing, stop talking, and freeze. *No one* could move until the nuns blew their whistles, which meant we could carefully, and slowly, walk back to class. I tried not to make any noise but it hurt so bad. I kept crying, and thinking, "Blow the whistle already so I can get some help!"

They *finally* blew their whistles. An older friend of our family - who was also a student - came over and helped me walk to the office. The nun in the office looked for cuts and/or bruises on my shoulder and elsewhere. She saw none, but she did notice my clothes were dirty (because I was pushed to the dirty ground!) and dusted me off. Wow, thanks. She then added, "Your fine," and sent me back to class. I was still crying from the pain.

After continuing to cry for a few more minutes, and being told to "be quiet" numerous times, my nun/teacher sent me *back to the office*. Once again, the nun still couldn't find anything wrong. They decided to call my mom. Yes, call my mom! But the nun calling couldn't get a hold of my mom.

It turned out Mom was vacuuming. Finally, she arrived at school and took me to the Emergency Room - another 20 minutes away. After some wait, I was taken to a bed/room. The doctor had my shoulder x-rayed which showed a broken left collar bone! Finally, I, and everyone, knew what was wrong with my shoulder. I wasn't crying for nothing!

By this time it had been over two hours since the actual break occurred. But now they had to reset the bone because it was a nasty fracture. So they put me out and wrestled it back into place.

There is no cast for a broken collar bone, just a football "shoulder pad" looking thing. I know what you're thinking, "Hey, at least you got to miss some school, and watch T.V." Nope! With only 3 channels back then, the only shows on T.V. in 1971 during the day were soap operas - and my mom, like every woman, LOVED them! Besides, I only got to miss two school days.

I don't remember what, if anything, ever happened to that bully.

According to the CDC: 4,400 kids die each year from bullying – that's more than 12 kids a day! That is an absolute failure of our society.

National Suicide Prevention Lifeline Phone Number:
1 800 273-8255
https://suicidepreventionlifeline.org

It was in third grade when I started noticing I had a tough time learning. I always finished assignments last and I worried myself sick over those speed tests for adding & subtracting, and multiplication tables. Not with memorizing what 6 x 7 equaled, I knew that was 43 – kidding, I'm kidding! I constantly confused the instructions. If my teacher said to add, I would multiply. If my teacher said multiply, I would subtract or add. It was frustrating and embarrassing. Kids picked on me and said I was "dumb", which made me sad - and angry. Lucky for me, my teacher would grade my work based on what I did, not what I was supposed to do.

During this time in my life I remember conversations coming up now and then regarding something called Polycystic Kidney Disease (PKD). I really didn't know what a kidney was and I didn't care; I was a kid with fun things to think about and do. Apparently some *old* people in our family had died from PKD. There was talk that Mom had it, especially since some of her family members had suffered and/or died from it. But to me, the six members of our family *seemed* healthy - so no big deal, right?

I did have *terrible* eczema growing up. No one knew why. I later did ask if it was because of "that PKD disease thing?" Our doctor didn't know. I went to our general M.D. constantly but there was no eczema creams, or prescriptions, back then. My feet and toes itched so bad. They would crack and bleed. I learned to walk around - in or out of shoes - with my toes sticking up in the air - they hurt so much. Nothing would help me. I just learned to put up with it for many years. I don't even remember how it healed itself, or exactly when, but it did clear up when I was an adult.

I was around 8 years old when one day I was sitting on my bottom with my legs tucked back behind my knees. Without any warning, something behind my left knee locked and an excruciating sharp pain ripped through my knee and body. I didn't know what it was happening but I somehow knew to instinctually kick my leg straight to "unlock" my knee, which stopped the pain. I told my parents but I could never quite explain what specifically happened, and the excruciating feeling. It would happen a few more time when I sat that certain way so I learned not to sit like that.

To this day, the thought of the pain gives me chills. And it still occurs occasionally - even after meniscus surgery (I'll talk about later). In fact, if I see our girls sitting that way I ask them to change the position of how they are sitting.

I bring some of these painful situations up not to say, "Oh, poor Rob", but because in the 1970's we knew little about PKD. And no one knew why I was having these health issues. Now that we know more about the disease I wonder if they're somehow related? PKD has such a big impact on how the entire body functions. I also wonder if others with PKD have had similar circumstances/conditions during their childhoods or beyond? People with any kind of chronic disease, not just kidney disease, tend to discuss the *major* issues they face, or faced, but often the "smaller", "nagging" things, like I mentioned above, aren't talked about, or are considered "insignificant".

But no matter how bad something hurt it didn't matter when I played baseball. I played with friends in the neighborhood and I also played many years on The City of Walnut baseball little league. But 'back in the good old days', you actually had to *earn* a trophy, and the only way to do that was to win the championship game. We came in 2nd place a few years, but NO TROPHY. Then, it happened. I was eleven years old. It came down to the last game of the season, and the last out. If we won = trophy! If we lost = nothing - again.

Well, we won the game! A few days later we got handed a trophy during a ceremony. It was only 7 or 8 inches tall, but I, we as a team, had *earned* it. And that remains one of my best memories ever.

When the fight begins within oneself,
a person is worth something.

~ Robert Browning ~

Left A Vegetable

Our family had been looking for a bigger home for months; four kids were only getting bigger. Just after I turned 9, mom and dad surprised us by telling us they had bought a new house – the house we all wanted. Everyone was so excited!

We would come home from school and pack up our rooms. But more and more my brother and I noticed our sisters had written "Fragile. Handle with care" on most of their boxes. What!? That's not fair! So, to make it fair, guess what we did? Yep. We wrote "FRAGILE. HANDLE WITH CARE" in big letters on almost every box. "So there!" we thought proudly. I even wrote those words on the box I put my pillow in! Oh, sibling rivalry.

We moved into our beautiful new home on October 2, 1974. Just ten days later - because that's how the the world works - Mom developed a severe headache. She said she was sick and went upstairs to lie down. After some time her headache got much worse. All of us could hear her now *screaming*. Dad decided to get Mom to the Emergency Room. I cried when I saw Dad help Mom - crying from the pain - carefully down the stairs and into the car that Saturday night. I felt so helpless, and alone.

Hours went by, as we waited for a call. Again, no cell phones back then. We, the kids, now lead by my oldest sister, who was only 13 herself (she didn't turn 14 until that December), didn't know what to do. I know I prayed to Jesus to make my mom better and to help all of us. I went to bed that night alone and scared not knowing what had happened.

I woke the next morning realizing the nightmare was real. Dad was home and he told us Mom was in "ICU". "ICU?", I asked, "What's that!?" He explained, "ICU, means Intensive Care Unit. They put people there who are really sick." He went on to tell us Mom had "a massive stroke = a blood vessel in her brain burst, causing bleeding in her brain." He called it a "cerebral hemorrhage", caused by, you guessed it, Polycystic Kidney Disease.

We do know today that PKD causes aneurysms which can lead to hemorrhaging. PLEASE get checked immediately for an aneurysm if you, or someone you love, has Polycystic Kidney Disease. This is critical as you'll learn more on this later.

Mom was just 35 years young. Her operation took over 5 hrs. What I didn't find out until many, many years later, was that the doctors warned Dad that night that his wife, our mom, would probably not survive. In fact, her heart did stop - twice – once as they rushed her into the operating room before surgery started. They rushed my dad out at that point. And the other time in the operating room during the brain surgery. The fantastic doctors were able to get her heart pumping again and save her life once again. I knew my mom was tough and this was just more proof. Dad told us the doctors told him the cerebral hemorrhage left mom "a complete vegetable", and that she would _never_ be much more than that; alive - but not capable of much of anything more.

She would be in Intensive Care for a week. We, the four kids, could finally see her the following Saturday after she was transferred to a regular room. We walked into the hospital and into that scary hospital room. Mom was hooked up to all these different machines, some making strange noises, some flashing lights, and others giving or receiving strange fluids. She was a mess. "Is that my mom?," I asked myself. I did what I could to not cry. I just stood there - in shock. And then with great difficulty, she opened her eyes and mumbled to us, "Who are you?"

What!?

Here I was, just a nine year old little boy wanting to hug, and get a hug from my mom. I went numb. She no longer knew who we were, who I was!? I wanted to scream, "We're your kids! Don't you remember us!? How come you don't remember me!?" She had no memory. She could barely talk, she couldn't read, and she had very limited motor skills. The once strong woman - who always got straight A's, and won essay contests, was a wife, and a mother of four, was in a matter of minutes reduced to some bones, organs, and skin, and a slightly functioning brain.

I then realized the top half of her head was wrapped in white gauze. Dad would later tell us doctors also had to temporarily remove part of her skull to relieve the swelling.

She was in the hospital for over a month.

She was released just before Thanksgiving. Thank God Mom was alive. We had so much to be thankful for.

But we also had no idea what was ahead for the six of us.

I would also find out much later that Mom did not want to go to the *new* house we had recently moved into when she was released from the hospital. She told Dad she wanted to "go home" which meant our *old* house - the house she somehow, slightly remembered. She didn't know anything about the new house.

The new owners of our old house *graciously* let my mom and dad in. Can you imagine what must have been going through their heads: "You want to come into our new home, the home you used to own, because your wife is sick???" My mom apparently just sat there for some time not saying a word, just looking around. Only The Good Lord knows what was trying to process through her damaged mind. She was probably thinking something was wrong since none of her things were there.

My anger grew the more I thought about what had happened. It wasn't fair! I asked God, "What did she do to deserve this?" She had already had a very difficult childhood – a time when a kid should just have fun trying to grow up. Now she had her own four kids (14, 12, 9, 7) - the first one almost killed her. And we were just supposed to be having our own fun trying to grow up.

I don't remember any big rah-rah family meeting where my dad huddled us up and said, "We're going to do this as a team – together!" We just learned to take one day at a time. And as you can imagine, there was (or is) no book written on how to handle this new life. We all had chores to do, and now we would have *a lot more* "chores" to do. As far as we knew from what we were told by all the doctors, Patricia Ann Herman was going to be a big lump of nothing that would need to be cared for 24/7, just like a newborn - adult sized baby - for as long as she lived. And she was just 35.

Honestly, looking back, I don't know how we did it, but we just did it, alone, and together as a family. The family history of kids running a household was repeating itself: John Jr. took care of his siblings; my mom took care of her siblings; and my oldest sister Laura was taking care of the three of us. But we four kids, and Dad, were going to be taking care of our mom and each other. What other choice did we have – put her in some *home* and let her rot away all alone? I don't think that possibility ever entered Dad's mind.

I never thought about it at the time, or sadly even during the many very trying years that followed, but how did my dad, at age 36 work full-time, manage himself, and now what was FIVE kids - two teenage girls, two young boys, and one woman who was a grown person but couldn't do anything for herself, insurance companies, doctor visits, a new house – that needed complete landscaping and other things, and the all the medicines? I guess that is the true definition of a "man". His incredible fortitude, and attitude, was/is a big part of what I think drives me to be so independent and to try to do everything myself.

Dad came up with the idea to place word signs everywhere, on everything: words like drawer, refrigerator, cupboard, table, chair, cup, plate, and on and on. It taught Mom to associate things with words. We constantly made her say words over and over. Slowly, day after day, month after month, and year after year, did my mom begin to say more words, and then short sentences. Besides speech and physical therapy classes, we all worked at helping her pronounce words, reading to her, reminding her of events like vacations we took, friends she knew, places she used to go. But it was tough trying to get her to remember things from 5 minutes ago, let alone 5 years or more ago. Doctors said her memory from her past was gone. We wanted to believe it was in her mind just somewhere locked away.

In addition to dealing with everything to that point, Dad's mom, Baba- who we loved and adored - had come out to be with us in Southern California. She needed lung cancer treatments from The City of Hope. Baba lost her cancer battle just one year after Dad's wife, my mom, became ill. I believe, at that point, we all stopped internally screaming, "What else could *possibly* happen!???", because we were too afraid of the answer.

Mom became increasingly frustrated with herself over time, over the years. It seemed she knew what she wanted, and had to do, but just couldn't. She would spend three long years in speech and physical therapy. But she Never Gave In! One day, someone in our family gave Mom a funny card with some cartoon bunnies on the front of it and on the inside. She became mad at herself because she couldn't read the card. Someone read the card to her and she muttered, "That's what I feel like - a dumb bunny."

From that point forward she would repeatedly call herself, "A dumb bunny." It may sound cute, but it was very sad and difficult to watch this once very strong woman become so angry because she couldn't do much of anything. I can never forget the feeling of helplessness as she mentally beat herself up. I always played it off, but inside I was infuriated with all of it. Dumb Bunny to her was a self-abusing term but we worked to make it into a positive, adorable, little fluffy creature. "Dumb Bunny", along with, "Did you take your pills?" were the constant battle cries in the Herman household.

The five of us tried, but admittingly it became apparent, no one really wanted to read to, and/or teach Mom to read, or even help her much in general. The month-after-month monotonousness was taking us down while we were trying to build her back up. Looking back, I don't know what else we could have done. My sisters wanted, and had, their own lives at 17 and 15. We all argued over who was to do what with Mom. My internal resentment, towards everyone, and everything, only grew worse.

The family was no longer a cohesive team with this one monumental goal. We all had our own goals: school, after school sports/drill team, homework, friends, activities. And we were all at, or getting to, that age where we wanted to grow up and move away from our parental control. And especially for me, a middle child at twelve, who had my big sisters acting as my mom, telling me what to do, and not do. I already had anger issues, issues with the littlest things bothering me, and not feeling capable.

We even tried going to counseling, but I was too afraid to speak up truthfully. There was no real communicating. It was always, "parents" speak at you telling you what to do and then you do it. So growing up I never knew I could do – be - anything I wanted. I always thought - 'I'm born and then my life is on some predetermined, uncontrolled-by-me, path.' It sure had been to that point in my crazy life.

My brother and I seemed to receive most of my dad's wrath. We did do stupid things but what young boys don't? If you have boys you can relate. Don't tell anyone but we did play with fire - in the house - with our friends. I know, very dumb! But when you don't have a mom, or you have three wanna-be mom's, a crazy-busy dad, and you're stuck inside the body of a pre-pubescence middle child, life tends to fly off in many different directions. I just *desperately* wanted somebody's love and attention!

Helping Mom always seemed to fall back on me. I didn't *want* to read to my mom anymore, or help her read anymore; I felt I *had to*, because she was my mom, and no one else would do it. I have always carried a huge sense of guilt of not being able to help Mom more, especially when she was berating herself. Helping Mom was one big daunting task and I, ashamedly, *hated* it. It also made me mad that my sisters and brother had stopped helping her. Mom was supposed to be teaching me stuff! I was supposed to be playing, doing homework - just trying to grow up.

School was a welcomed relief from the craziness at home - time when I could just be a normal kid. I went to school late in sixth grade - it was a weird schedule - so I was home, alone, with Mom during the mornings. Before Dad went off to work, he would warn me about Mom's 'mini strokes'. What!? I'm only eleven years old!

If you have ever seen someone go through a transient ischemic attack (TIA), a mini stroke, you know it's a scary, disturbing experience. I would watch Mom lie on the ground, on her side, shaking violently, not being able to talk, sometimes drooling, while I tried to hold her still so she wouldn't hurt herself. After about a minute or so (which seemed like ten minutes) it would stop. It is not something that any young person should *ever* have to see their parent go through.

And my being angered by things continued, and only just got worse. I remember being *angry* not being able to watch what I wanted to watch on T.V., or that my sisters boyfriend would come over and sleep on the floor while we all watched T.V. Or not wanting anything to do with my sisters friends when they came over. Or when we had to go in the kids from the neighborhood would stay sitting on our front grass; them sitting on *our* grass drove me crazy. I don't know why I was like that. And I had no outlet, or release, no escape, from my physical world, nor my mental world.

God is with those who patiently persevere.
~ Arabian Proverb ~

Cancer

In seventh and eighth grade I attended Suzanne Jr. High School. I played on the school's flag football team both years. I made the all star team both years. I loved playing wide receiver on offense, and cornerback on defense. But the best part was just being part of a positive, fun experience.

I also won the Presidential Fitness Award both years. And I even made the Honor Roll but it was not easy; I had to spend *a lot* of time studying when I wasn't helping with Mom. It wasn't from being smart, it was from the pressure from my parents to always do well in school, especially since my oldest sister, Laura, always got straight A's. Thanks a lot sis!

Being stuck in the middle (child) was also frustrating. I started to steal from my teachers, from friends, and then from stores. Maybe it was to be cool and/or an attempt to get more attention. I was Catholic. I knew it was very wrong. One time I stole a candy bar. It was my brother's and my favorite. I showed it to him. I don't know why I showed him – except to get his attention or to be the cool big brother? Then I *begged* him not to tell and ended up giving him almost the entire candy. And then what did he do?

First, he told my sister-mom Laura, who scolded me, and made me say prayers – Our Fathers and Hail Marys. Then, yep, he told my dad! This was not the first time I had stolen and my dad found out so let's just say my punishment was – extreme - and painful. But I never stole again, so lesson learned.

In July of 1977, 12 inches of rain fell on Johnstown, PA in 24 hours causing the Second great flood and killing 84 people. Ten feet of water covered my mom's mom's house! (Yes, the non-nice Baba.) So that October my dad used his/our vacation time to fly to Pennsylvania for a week to help rebuild Baba's home - because that's the type of man Robert J. Herman is.

Just after returning from that trip my dad noticed a spot on his foot. Dad, who was only 39 years old at the time was diagnosed with malignant melanoma on the top of his right foot. It was also just 3 years since mom's hemorrhage.

Cancer!

What!? I went with him to one of his many doctor visits before his surgery. The nurse gave him some kind of shot in the top of his foot, probably for a biopsy. It was the first time I had truly seen my dad in pain, in agony and it scared me. I thought, first my mom was taken away from me, and now my dad would be taken too. I couldn't have been more confused - was I supposed to be angry at God - or just sit helplessly in my room and cry?

The following month Dad had surgery. To remove all of the cancer they removed most of the skin from the top of his foot. It was grotesque. (See the picture in the back of the book under "Area 51".) He couldn't walk on it for a week.

Weeks later surgeons took skin from his behind and used it to cover the top of his foot.

I was lost more than ever. But, I was still somehow *persevering.*

*He who commits a wrong will himself
inevitably see the writing on the wall, though
the world may not count him guilty.*

~ Martin Tupper ~

Oh, It Gets Sicker!

This part of my story I thought a lot about not including. It is deeply personal and can still be upsetting. But with this book, I am trying to convey that regardless of your life's circumstances: being bullied, being a young caretaker of an ill parent, and/or as you'll discover later, being subjected to numerous physical and mental health challenges myself, whatever you face, I overcame it all, and you can too. You are not alone, because I believe being alone, feeling alone, is the worst feeling of all. But please remember horrible things can, and probably will, happen to you yet you can still have the most incredible, blessed life.

Around the same time of all the craziness of Mom getting sick is when I can remember my dad's brother, Uncle Tom, began doing *inappropriate* things to me.* *Molesting* is the appropriate word.

He was also doing things to others. Once in a while I talked with the other persons about what Uncle Tom was doing to us - but never specifics. I did not want to know what happened to them, unless they wanted to tell me. And I did not/do not want anyone to know what specifically happened to me. After all, those details are not what's important here. But just like my mom's stroke took a piece of my heart, my uncle took an even bigger piece of my soul. By eleven years old, I didn't realize it, but I was a very messed up kid.

After a few *years*, one day I decided I *had* to finally tell my parents. You're probably wondering why I didn't say anything after the FIRST incident but it's critical to understand I was scared of saying, or doing, anything wrong to our parents.

Speaking only for myself, there was no open, two way, communication. I was already timid; not sure if I was born that way, or it developed later via ongoing circumstances; at the very least, it was compounding itself. I just did what I was told. I never dreamed of asking "Why?", or "How come?" And we never had any deep, connecting discussions about life, politics, religion, shows on T.V., school, the sports teams I was on, my likes or dislikes, including girls.

Oh, and if you're wondering if my parents ever gave me the "birds and the bees" talk, you tell me. Here's how it went: Parents - "Rob, we want to talk to you about girls. Do you know about girls?" Me - "Yes, I know about girls", incredibly embarrassed. Parents - "Do you know you're not supposed to touch girls breasts?" Me - "Yes, I know I shouldn't touch girls breasts.", furiously embarrassed! Parents - "OK, good."

And that was it.

Someone should have told my dad's brother to not touch young boys!

I thought I would be blamed, not Dad's brother, who my dad seemed to love very much. I always hoped and prayed someone would see him/us, so I wouldn't have to say anything; the police could just come and put him away.

In the downstairs entry way in our house, I knew had to find the courage to *finally* tell my parents. Today was *the* day. I was so nervous and afraid. My parents were watching T.V. in our den. I stood in the doorway. I started to cry as I said, "I need to talk to you about something. Uncle Tom has been touching me." "Touching you... where?", my dad asked. "Down there," pointing to my privates.

They didn't say anything.

Seconds ticked by that seemed like long minutes...

In my head I thought, "I think he went back to watching T.V. How long do I stand here?" So, thinking I was now going to be in really big trouble any moment, I turned and quietly left the room, and went upstairs.

That was it.

They must have gone back to watching TV because neither my mom or dad – EVER - said anything about Uncle Tom: not that night, the next morning, the next visit from Uncle Tom, ever. Oh, yes, he still came around. (Though coincidently, or not, Uncle Tom seemed to visit less often.) I didn't talk about 'it' again.

To this day, I'm not sure if I ever felt more alone than at that time.

If you or someone you know is being abused physically, mentally, sexually, please reach out for help...immediately... to stop it.

Childhelp National Child Abuse Hotline
https://www.childhelp.org/hotline
1-800-4-A-CHILD (1-800-422-4453)

The Childhelp National Child Abuse Hotline is open 24 hours a day, 7 days a week. All calls are confidential.

After that, it's sad for me to say, I lost a huge amount of my respect for my dad – my teacher of many good things.

It had always ripped another piece of my heart away knowing my dad or mom did absolutely NOTHING to protect their own, innocent, children! I was 13ish when I *finally* was brave enough to say something. Mom was still recovering from her stroke so I didn't expect anything from her. But Dad, the strong one, the supposed family protector, had on numerous occasions made it clear he had it in him to get mad.

It wouldn't be until I was around 45 years old when somehow the topic of Uncle Tom came up in some conversations with my sisters, and I mentioned him molesting me. Laura, the oldest, didn't say much, which made me very upset. But Janice was mad. FINALLY, someone who stood up for me! For once, I didn't feel so alone with that heavy burden.

My sister did ask another family member about their interactions with Uncle Tom, and apparently *many* in the Herman family knew he liked little boys. Most of the males at some point had been "approached". I was shocked! And I was now even more angry!! Why would anyone allow this to happen over, and over, and over to innocent helpless kids!?

My sister later asked Dad about the infamous day when I told him and he said he, "had no recollection of it". What!? How could he not remember his kid crying, telling him his own brother is molesting his own child? Why then did he ask that night, "Touching you... where?"

Final Note: It is sad that Uncle Tom used a gun to commit suicide. There were days when I wished he would have done it before he met me. I never understood the true meaning of *forgiveness* until writing this part of my story. If someone is hurting inside so bad that they would *ever even think* of killing themself, let alone actually do it, that's pain I don't wish on anyone, anymore. Because as you'll soon read, I know that type of pain. And that's exactly why I wrote the lyrics to "Suicide". More on this coming soon.

Nothing in life is more wonderful than faith - the one great moving force which we can neither weigh in the balance nor test in the crucible.

~ Sir William Osler ~

"Your Spine Is Curved"

As you know by now the years after Mom's massive stroke were "confusing", to put it mildly. During the years of her recovery, as she got better, one of the toughest things was she wanted to still be the parent, in control of everything/me. So on one hand I was still helping her learn how to function again, while on the other she was desperately trying to tell me what to do and how to do it, even though she really couldn't. Does that make sense? It often feels so difficult to get anyone to relate to all of this. How could you if you haven't been through it yourself? It was a crazy, difficult, incredibly frustrating, continuous, dilemma for me. And, I was trying to grow up, going through puberty and all the fun that brings.

Let me share just one example with you of what I mean. My mom let me go over to my friend's house but I could not to go inside since no parent was home. Scott lived at the other end of our long street and Mom had a neighbor friend over. Well, long story short, my mom leaves her guest, in our house, while she walked all the way down the street. Next thing I know my mom is at the gate *screaming* for me. I came out front and we walked home. She was mad. I started thinking about my punishment. At least, I was too old to be spanked, right?

Once home, mom immediately got the wooden spoon out of the drawer - *pulled down my pants* - and spanked the 'crud' out of my naked bottom - all in front of our neighbor!! And I was 13!!!*

The humiliation; any dignity I had was now gone. I think that was sort of the last straw. Instead of growing up, I was shutting down. It all just became too much. I actually began thinking of putting an end to all my physical and mental torment.

I started ninth grade when I was fourteen at Walnut High School. I tried out for the basketball team that Fall. This was the first time I was required to pass a sports physical. This was when I was first exposed to "the cough", when they check for a hernia (which I would have many in my life... hernias; more on that later). So, no hernias, but my doctor did ask me, "Do you know your spine is curved?" I responded, "No. What does that mean?"

After another doctor visit and some x-rays, it meant, scoliosis. What!?

I had a 46 degree curve in my spine!

Growing up prior to mom's hemorrhage, my mom would always make us stand against a wall with our shoulders back for good posture so I always wondered what happened. In actuality though, bad posture has little, to no, bearing on why people develop scoliosis. But less than 1% of the individuals with scoliosis require surgery. Yea me!

What role did PKD play? I know other people have scoliosis and PKD, but is it coincidental or related? My brother was always healthy and still is perfectly healthy. He has never a broken bone, never any surgery, never any migraines, never any eczema - and he does NOT have PKD; the only one out of the four children. And trust me, my health issues are just getting started.

(Come to think of it, my siblings are smart... and they were NOT dropped on their heads as babies! Hmmm??? Thanks again sis!)

Things turned serious for me. After more doctor visits with specialists I was given a choice: wear a brace and perform back exercises for the rest of my life so it didn't get worse - it would never get better. Or have a metal - Harrington - rod surgically fused/attached to the top and bottom of my spine vertebrae to straighten it back to as normal as possible. I remember becoming woozy, almost fainting, while the doctors explained all the gory surgery details. It had only been five years since Mom's stroke, and just two years since Dad's cancer, and now my own surgery was approaching.

Surgery was scheduled for the morning after Christmas so I would miss less school since I was going to be in a body cast for 6 months! It was a family tradition that on Christmas Eve we would open the present from the family member who had your name. But this Christmas I also got to open just *one* present from "Santa". (I would be in the hospital for at least a week recovering so why couldn't I open them all!???) I had wanted a blue remote controlled car and I knew the box. I opened the gift - the blue car! Yes! "Wait! Where are the... Are you kidding me? Someone forgot the batteries!"

I tried to stay positive, but I was so angry.

My sister's boyfriend was eventually able to bring us some batteries before my Christmas Eve was over.

Christmas was terrible that year as I did my best to tell everyone I was not worried or scared about my surgery. But even while opening presents that Christmas morning all I could think about was what was going to be happening to me later in the day. The only thing I knew about hospitals and surgery was the nightmare of Mom's, and Dad's, experiences.

I checked into the hospital that evening Christmas Day. I was taken to my room, dressed in a gown, and climbed into a bed. After some time, my parents left. No, no one stayed the night with me. I was alone - again.

I was watching T.V. when an older, but very nice, nurse came in and gave me some instructions about something I had, she had, to do. She spoke in broken english and I couldn't understand what she was telling me. She handed me a box to read and rolled me onto my side. Just as I looked at the picture and read some of the instructions, something was placed up my rectum. "Dear Lord, what is she doing to me!???" Then the weirdest, strangest part... a bunch of, what felt like some kind of liquid, was squirted into my behind!* What was going on!? And why would someone do this to a fourteen year old whose life already stinks because... HE'S IN THE HOSPITAL... ON CHRISTMAS DAY... WAITING TO HAVE MAJOR BACK SURGERY THE NEXT MORNING!???

My first enema.

Well, at least running to the bathroom all night kept my mind off being alone and the next day's coming "fun".

Before I knew it I woke up and they told me the surgery was over. I had no cast on so I wasn't sure. I now had an I.V. in my right arm. I was told to just lie still on my back and to not move around much. The surgery went well, and I had – and still have - a fourteen inch scar running down the middle of my back. I was also reminded by one of the nurses that I would have this stainless steel for the rest of my life.

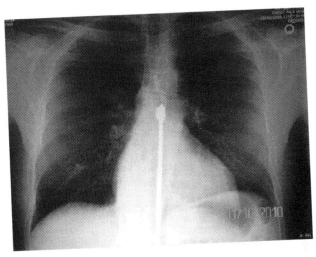

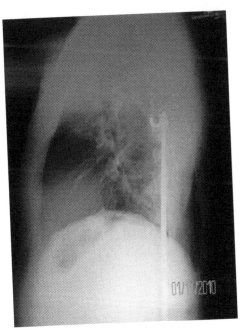

And my back does not/cannot bend like a normal back. All of my bending comes from the hips. My back stays perfectly straight, which is why I sit up so straight. I remember my nervousness the first time I had to go through a metal detector. No, I did not set it off it off!

The next day my I.V. was changed and moved to my lower right wrist area. I hadn't noticed but when the nurse came in to check on me hours later she noticed I had a large bump next to my I.V. "What is happening!?", I nervously thought. Apparently, the I.V. was not in my vein. I was told the liquid would be absorbed by my body, and "not to worry". They say that to you a lot in the hospital.

The following day I would have my body cast put on though I was still extremely sore. My cast ran from under my armpits and up to the base of my throat, down to the middle of my hips. It took some time to get over the feeling of claustrophobia. I felt like I was trapped in a tight cage with pressure on my chest when I expanded my lungs to take deep breaths. I was on my back, feeling like a turtle when it's on its back.

For a number of days I could do nothing but lay there. I was not to get out of bed for any reason, especially without help. Back then doctors didn't stress walking soon after surgery. I do remember trying to walk after about a week flat on my back – my legs were so weak I had a tough time standing, let alone walking.

If you are wondering how I went to the bathroom, well, let me tell you how. To go #1, I had a plastic water jug; not comfortable, not natural, not easy! To go #2, yikes! I had to call the nurse. She would bring in a bed pan and place it under my bottom and then tell me it was ok to go. Can you visualize this??? I am fourteen, laying on my back, my legs bent holding my bottom up with the pan underneath me - that the nurse is holding in place - with all my nakedness exposed trying to poop! Good Lord, what did I do to deserve all this fun!? At least, I didn't need another enema.

I spent New Year's 1980 in the hospital and was released a few days later, for a total of ten nights. I would be taking sponge baths for the next six long months. And I used various sticks and hangers to reach my itches. Baby powder was my best friend because it gets hot in Southern California and I was *sweaty,* and *stinky.*

It wasn't until I got home in normal surroundings that I realized that by straightening my spine the doctors had stretched me up almost 5 inches taller to about 6' 1". (I am 6' 2" today.) I was thin already, but this made me rail thin.

My doctors and parents repeatedly warned me to be careful, and absolutely no sports! I was told I would damage my spinal surgery and/or cause very serious injuries, including permanent paralysis. But as a fourteen year old, very active young man - did I listen? Nope, which was *really* dumb. I loved basketball. I played basketball at lunch when I went back to high school. And, of course, I took a few hard falls playing. And I even got into a brief fight. The guy probably broke his hand on my body cast! The Good Lord was definitely watching over me over those months.

Clothing with a body cast was also a problem. My pants did not fit around my waist due to the width of the cast, so my parents gave me a pair of my dad's pants. Oh, boy! I was now taller than my dad so his pants were not long enough. That was one embarrassing fashion statement.

Six months and no pants to fit me. Our family was always very money conscious so I never wanted to spend their money wastefully. I decided to wear - to school, church, almost everywhere - that one pair of tan pants everyday. So just imagine: being a *freshman* in high school, having to wear a body cast for 6 months, in your dad's pants, and being rail thin. Could I be anymore attractive to girls!???

Somehow, I still kept up with my studies. My life was a constant battle with 'doing what I had to do'. It was during my recovery that I asked my parents for a crucifix – a cross, to wear around my neck. And I specifically asked for a cross with Jesus on it, so that I, and everyone who sees it, will remember the tortures of our Savior's final days before dying on that cross. I needed to tell myself what I had gone through in my life up unto that point was nothing compared to what Christ endured. It allowed me to press onward. The chains have changed over the years, but I still wear that same wonderful cross. You'll notice it in some of the pictures.

The cast drove me crazy. By the time June came around, I, and it, stunk so bad. I had over the months put holes in the cast to let it breathe better. The holes got bigger and bigger over time, while I also picked pieces of the cast off. I was done with ninth grade and done with my cast.

Hallelujah.

Bring on summer!

The greatest mistake you can make in life is to be continually fearing you will make one.

~ Elbert Hubbard ~

Is This Normal, Or Is It Just Me?

At this point in time, it was six years mom since mom was diagnosed by her doctors as a lifelong "vegetable", and that she would *never* be anything more. Physically and mentally she was so much better. Every day she was proving them all wrong. She could now make some dinners, clean, go for walks, even go shopping, and most importantly to her, go to church; she even cleaned the church. She could even read her bible, slowly, on her own again. In fact, she held mini bible gatherings in our home for anyone she could get to join her. She always made it very clear it was her faith in Jesus Christ that was pulling her through her miraculous recovery. I know she was a miracle. All of her doctors were now saying she is a miracle.

With mom "better", Dad outside of work, always stayed busy with some project. But he would also take us and our friends places, like the beach (my favorite is Corona Del Mar Beach in So Cal), so we all could go boogie boarding and body-surfing. One day he took us to the mountains to play in the snow. There was nowhere to play because it was so crowded. It doesn't snow much in Southern California so you have to go to the mountains to feel the white stuff. We stopped on the side of a road to do some exploring. My brother, our friends Frank and Chuck, and I, found a small patch of open snow on a hill. If you're thinking nothing good is going to come of this - you are correct!

Everything happened so fast from there. Chuck started to slip. I tried to help, and the next thing I realized, Chuck is gone! He flew down the slope, and then so did I. I remember being so scared as I flew down the mountain on my bottom, going through brush that repeatedly slapped me in the face. Then I smacked into - and up - a big tree. I spun up and around the tree, landed hard, and kept going.*

I was knocked out.

When I woke, my dad was right there. Unbeknownst to me at the time, Dad got two ropes from a rescue crew and worked his way down to where I was laying. Dad asked me where Chuck was. I told him, "I don't know. I think he's down there somewhere," pointing farther down the mountain. I was staring at good 500 feet or more to the road and our car.

Somehow I, and eventually Chuck and my dad, made it back up to where Frank and my brother were. No one had any outside bleeding so we drove home. But at home my face was cut up and my bottom had turned BLACK, with some purples and blues. I had never seen anything like it and neither had my parents. It was Sunday so the next day we went to our doctor. It took weeks to heal but I had another incredible story. (No, I don't have a picture of my bottom from then!)

It wasn't long after that brush with fate when I started my first official job, being hired at a fast food restaurant, making $3.35 an hour. I was seventeen and a good friend of mine worked there. My fellow co-workers and I would host parties at someone's house and charge people to come in. (We did almost anything to make some money.) During one party, I drank too much alcohol. DUMB, I know. I had to open the restaurant the next morning, but I couldn't – I was sooo sick. My first hangover. And, it would be my only hangover. It hurt sooo bad! I asked myself, "How do people get drunk and still function the next day?" That day I swore I would NEVER get drunk again. Lesson learned.

I graduated from Walnut High School... with honors... at age 17. Yeah, I don't know how I did it either! My senior year routine was to get up early, walk 3/4 of a mile to school where I worked out so hard in gym class before lunch I would almost faint. Then I would not have a lunch to eat because I was too tired in the morning to make a lunch. I would walk home, do homework, and then off to work until 11:00 closing. I would arrive at home around midnight after closing down the restaurant. I also worked 8 hour days on Saturday and Sunday. I got little sleep, and was always exhausted. But somehow I managed to get a whole lot out of 24 hours. My crazy work ethic was more refined than ever. It provided a focus forward, and not that path from the past.

After graduation I bought my first car that summer just before I turned eighteen. It was the coolest black on black 1966 Ford Mustang Coupe, with a red stripe down low along the side. It had a painted blue, automatic 289 engine with a huge chrome air filter. It cost $4600 - all my savings, and a little more borrowed from Dad. Did that car get the right, and wrong, kind of attention and trouble? Yes, it sure did.

So I had my own car and a high school diploma; now what do I do? Growing up in a regimented home I didn't know what I wanted to do when I graduated. I didn't feel I was good at anything specific. To this day, I am envious of young people who know exactly what they want to do with their life. Mom always told my brother and I she, "prayed that at least one of her sons would become a priest." No pressure there.

I did know it was expected of me to go to college. My oldest sister went to college and she was "successful". Mt San Antonio Community College, located conveniently in my hometown, is where I started college. I paid for my classes by going full time during the day and working almost full time at night.

The restaurant closed at 11:00pm and then it took generally 1/2 hour to break down everything - clean the fryer, put all the food away, wash dishes, and sweep – making it ready for the next day. At the end of a long day all of us would want to go home as soon as possible so we would begin breaking everything down prior to closing if it wasn't busy.

One of my cleaning jobs was the french fryer.

Side note: The dirty grease was collected daily into a vat which was regularly collected by a company who sold the grease to cosmetic companies. Yep, that dirty grease was used to make make-up!

To clean the fryer I let it *cool* down, *drain* the grease, and then *scrub* the top and insides clean while wearing thick protective gloves. Well, one day I decided to start cleaning the fryer early around 10:00 pm – while it was still boiling hot. I was bent over, wearing a protective glove on my right hand, scrubbing the top area when my hand slipped into the dirty grease. In an instant, the boiling hot grease had splashed onto my face!*

At that time during my life I had a mustache, so luckily, a lot of the grease landed on it along with my nose, eyelids, cheeks, and chin area. I remember being initially stunned. Then my face began to excruciatingly burn. Surprisingly to me I calmly walked back to the sink and splashed cold water on my face. I don't know if that's the best thing to do for a burn, but it sure felt better at the time. My manager closed the restaurant. She was going to call 911 when I asked her to call my dad instead, who took me to the E.R.

Note: You should NOT put cold water on a burn, particularly second and third degree burns, because the cold water could cause you to go into shock, which could be fatal.*

I had some second and third degree burn marks on my face – something that got me some interesting looks when I went back to college and work the next week. The true blessing – no permanent scars.

It takes courage to live - courage and strength and hope.
And courage and strength and hope have to be bought
and paid for with pain and work and prayers and tears.

~ Jerome P. Fleishman ~

Mom's Dialysis

Almost ten years to the day of mom's massive cerebral hemorrhage, she took her drivers test and passed! She was 45 years old. It was a HUGE accomplishment, especially when stopping to really think about who she was before, then during her long, continuing recovery, to that very day when she was once again demeaned competent enough by the state to, at least, drive a car on the crazy streets of Southern California. Amazing! She was not and never would be again her old strong self. But now everyone agreed - she was no longer a vegetable - she was an absolute MIRACLE!

My mom _never gave in_.

With that accomplishment also came the reality her kidneys were noticeably failing, being overrun by many (poly) cysts. She was once again becoming weaker and weaker. She was also very cold all the time. Most of us with Polycystic Kidney Disease can relate to this annoying condition. As an example, we could never make her coffee, tea, or soup, hot enough. It had to literally be bubbling boiling hot before she would drink it. Truth be told, it tested our virtuous patience again, always trying to keep her, and her food, warm enough. I know it drove our waiter or waitress nuts having to continually heat and reheat her coffee to her specifications when we dined out.

We knew the day was coming soon when she would have to start dialysis, something she was not looking forward to. So before she would start dialysis Dad took Mom to the Holy Land for twelve days. It was a dream trip of Mom's and it gave her a boost of energy she truly needed.

I remember the debate we had as to what dialysis method would work best for her: hemodialysis- usually performed through graft or fistula, or peritoneal dialysis – performed through a catheter connected to a tube extending out and away from the body. Mom was opposed to having anything sticking out of her body because she felt it took away from her femininity.

So she had surgery for a fistula graft. An arteriovenous (AV) fistula is a type of access used for hemodialysis. It can be used whether dialysis is performed at a dialysis center, or you perform home hemodialysis (HHD). An AV fistula is a connection between an artery and a vein creating a ready source with a rapid flow of blood. Source: www.MayoClinic.org

If you have ever seen a fistula, or graft, they are generally not considered "pretty". In fact, they're what I call, "pretty, pretty ugly". (I'll share more about my own fistula surgery later.) Mom's veins and arteries were so small and fragile instead of trying to create a fistula they placed a rubber tube, called a graft, under her forearm skin and connected one end to a vein and the other end to an artery.

During this time Mom was informed by her doctors she would never qualify for a kidney transplant because of the many blood transfusions, and other complications she had over her challenging life. So Dad, myself, and my brother were trained on the dialysis equipment. Mom began dialyzing four times a week, at night, via hemodialysis, at home in her bed where she was most comfortable.

Dialysis would keep her alive for the rest of her life.

Did you know the first successful kidney dialysis was in 1945? Dutch Dr. Willem Kolff invented the first dialysis machine in 1943 after watching helplessly as a male patient died of kidney failure. Dr Kolff, in his research, found an article on removing toxins in animals written by Jon Abel in 1913. That article inspired Dr. Kolff to invent his machine. After a few unsuccessful attempts a 67 year old woman came out of a coma after eleven hours of dialysis. Life-saving success!

WWW.DAVITA.COM – THE HISTORY OF KIDNEY TRANSPLANTATION:

The first kidney transplant was attempted in Russia in 1933 using a kidney from a deceased individual. The first successful kidney transplant was on June 17, 1950. It was performed on Ruth Tucker, a 44 year old with Polycystic Kidney Disease. There were no immune suppression medications so the donated kidney only last 10 months. But that 10 months gave her existing kidney enough time to heal itself. She lived another five long years!

The first living transplant occurred in Paris in 1952 but only lasted three weeks.

And the first long term kidney transplant was performed in Boston in December 1954, between twin brothers, by Dr. Joseph Murray. Again, no immune suppression drugs but because they were twins there was little rejection risk. The recipient lived another eight long years!

And The PKD Foundation (www.pkdcure.org) was founded in 1982 by Dr. Jared J. Grantham and Dr. Joseph K. Bruening. Their sole purpose was/is to find a cure for Polycystic Kidney Disease. Its first research grant was awarded to my doctor, Dr. William Bennett, in the amount of $25,000.00. (More on Dr. Bennett later.)

*Sometimes what a man escapes to is
worse than what he escapes from.*

~ Stan Lynde ~

Movin' Out, Tryin' To Move On

One of my friends had gotten a job at an account reconcilement center for a bank. He told me they were hiring and I had my first *true* interview. I had no idea what to expect. I was eighteen. (The "internet" was just beginning in 1982 and only a few people had home computers.)

I got the job! I would now be working full time. So I changed my college classes to nights and kept working Saturday and Sunday during the day. I was never home. The bank also paid for my college classes. I was also introduced to this technology called a facsimile machine, or fax. You dialed a phone number and the person on the other end (of course they needed a fax machine also) received an exact replica of the information you had. Amazing!

Growing up Dad would talk about how he joined the military at 17 so I always felt this "pressure" to move out after high school. Most of my friends joined the military after high school but with my scoliosis they would not have taken me. Still 18, I told my parents I was moving out; I could, now that I had a full time, good paying job with benefits. Myself and two friends rented a house.

My move out date came. I showed up after work on a Saturday to move my things - I didn't have but an old desk, an old twin bed, and my clothes. But my parents weren't home. What!? Yes, they knew I was moving out that day. Now understand my parents RARELY went anywhere and suddenly they were gone, and they didn't tell me either. And they couldn't have gone far because at this point in time mom's PKD kidneys were getting worse. So I gathered up my things and left. I just knew I would do whatever I had to do to make it in the real world.

Never Give In!

My rented room was so small in the morning I would stand my twin mattress up against the wall to make room to move around. At the time, I didn't truly realize the gravity of moving out. Looking back it was probably an attempt to escape: an escape from all the memories of dealing with my mom's struggles; and my personal mental and physical struggles, including being molested.

My schedule was packed. I was on my own. It felt good but I knew I wasn't actually free from much. My migraines became more frequent. I had broken up with my longtime girlfriend which left me feeling heartbroken and lonely. So when I did have free time I started writing lyrics for songs. I love music and I thought it would be a great way express my feelings, frustrations, and heartbreak. I wrote lyrics/songs called, "Away", "Can't Say Goodbye", "Where Are We Today", and "Why Must I Cry". Other writings felt more like poetry, "Mirrors", "Why? (Arms That Destroy)", and "What You'll Never See In Me". If you're interested, I have included the words for a few songs, and poems, in the back of this book.

But the lyrics to... "Suicide"... were finished on 7/31/86 – just two weeks from my 21st birthday. MY 21st BIRTHDAY! (The lyrics are a little disturbing, but are in the back under "Area 51".) During a time when I had everything in front of me, I couldn't escape what was tormenting me from my yesterdays. I think over those prior years I had thought of every possible way to end it all. BUT, writing things down did help release *a few* of the demons.

PLEASE don't ever hurt yourself or someone else. No matter what, you are unique and very needed. Never be ashamed to reach out for help.

National Suicide Prevention Lifeline Phone Number

1 800 273-8255

https://suicidepreventionlifeline.org

or

for our military heroes...

The Veterans Crisis Help Line

1 800 273-8255 (press 1)

www.veteranscrisisline.net

I earned my two year AA Liberal Arts degree in Business Management from Mt San Antonio College. Now there were a number of prerequisite classes that had to be completed before earning that degree. One of those classes was "Public Speaking". Now up until this point for most of my schooling I generally did as little as possible when having to give an oral presentation; my fear was that powerful and I know I am not alone when I say that.

One of the presentations required allowed us to go outside and present on anything we wanted. I loved my 1966 Mustang so I presented my car. I began by showing her off inside and out. Then with everyone huddled around I told this incredible, absolutely true story:

(When this event happened I was still living at home.)

My 1966 Mustang was fast, and sometimes I drove it too fast, which was the case on that Saturday night. I was driving fast showing off around Diamond Bar before heading home around 11:00 pm. Walnut still had few street lights so most streets were very dark and had very few stores. As I turned onto La Puente Road I noticed four black guys in the middle of the road waving at me trying to get me to stop. We still had no cell phones back then. I needed to get home but I decided to stop to see if I could help. They were out of gas and there were no gas stations nearby. I told them I could drive someone to a gas station; they all got in. We drove a few miles to the nearest gas station which was closed because gas stations backed then closed by 11:00pm!

We drove back to their car and decided to push their car to somewhere - I don't remember where we were going to go but to at least get it off the road. I didn't want to damage my car going bumper-to-bumper so one guy got on the back of their car with his feet on my car. (Got a good visual?)

I then started to slowly push the car forward. The gap between the two cars widened a little and the next thing I know this guy dropped to the ground and under my car.

In an instant I realized, "I've run someone over!"

I slammed on the brake - *nothing* happens!!

In another instant I realize, "I have no brakes!"

I then immediately think to throw the moving car into reverse. I was going slow and my car began to drift backwards.

I was now in shock as I continued to slowly drift backwards not concerned if anything was behind me. It was now passed midnight so no one or cars, thank God, were around.

The guy on the ground that I ran over slowly got up and began yelling, "I'm ok, I'm ok!", but he didn't look that ok. He was limping.

But I have no brakes as I, again, while still moving put the car back in drive and began moving forward, back toward the guys who are all now yelling, "He's ok! He's ok! It's ok!"

Then the yelling changed to, "Don't go! Don't leave! Stop!, as I drove passed them, myself now yelling, "I have no brakes! I have no brakes! I can't stop!"

I decided I needed to get help myself, since I no longer had a way to stop. I drove as slow as I could through stop signs (there were no stop lights in our small town) and - thank God again - empty streets. I made it home and bumped my dad's car sitting in the driveway to stop.

I sat in my car in our driveway – stunned - by what had just transpired. I also said a good long "Thank you Jesus" prayer.

What caused the brakes to fail? My brother had worked on my brakes earlier in the day and did not "bleed" my brakes which is *critical* when fixing brakes. Bleeding the brakes removes any air pockets in the fluid lines. If you don't, you have what happened to me - your brakes fail.

During the next days following that fateful night it hit me what kind of trouble I could have been in if the brakes would have failed earlier when I was driving around crowded areas. Or what if I would not have stopped to help, or *try* to help, those stranded guys?* My Guardian Angel above was again looking out for me.

I still wonder what ever happened to those guys.

Oh, I got an "A+" on my presentation.

Perhaps they are not stars but, rather openings in Heaven where the love of our lost ones pours through and shines down upon us to let us know they are happy.

~ Eskimo Proverb ~

Take Her To Heaven

Mom's PKD kidneys continued to worsen as she continued her dialysis routine at home. On Thanksgiving of 1988, a little over 14 years after Mom's devastating cerebral hemorrhage, she suffered a series of seizures. Mom was now just 49 years old and apparently because someone up above thought she had not had enough she then had another stroke. This one left her paralyzed. Somehow though while in the hospital she shocked everyone when they found her – standing - next to her bed! She never, ever stopped fighting.

But she was still not out of the woods. The seizures and stroke had taken their toll and left her very fragile. She developed pneumonia. And because she spent so much time in that hospital bed, with incontinence, she developed horrible bed sores. I remember her regularly screaming from the immense pain as a nurse would have to wipe her privates after she went in a bedpan.

That screaming ripped me up inside and it destroyed a little more of my heart and soul. It reminded me of her screaming when she had her first stroke when I was nine.

I always wondered why someone couldn't invent a bed that had a small square door that opened under the person's bottom so they could go #1 and #2 into a catch basin. The bed sheet(s) would have to have an opening also and would also need to be of waterproof fabric. The opening would also allow (warm) water to be poured on the person's privates to help in the cleaning process. And speaking from personal experience, it would be a lot more comfortable than going in a bedpan. It would also be easier on the nurses to clean their patients. There's a multi-million dollar idea! I get royalties if someone uses my idea.

My mom was in so much pain that I grew more and more angry as I watched helplessly, particularly as one particular nurse didn't seem to care about the pain she was inflicting. Most of my life I had always prayed for Jesus to help her. But my prayers switched, and I begged for Him to stop all her pain by taking her to Heaven. She had suffered enough during her short, pain-filled life.

Mom turned 50 on January 7, 1989. Her final stroke was on Saturday, January 28, which left her on life support. She fought until February 4 – twenty five years to the day her and Dad arrived in California - ending a torturous life, not deserved.

It was over. She could finally rest and find the peace she always aspired to feel.

Now, I'm fairly certain no one *likes* funerals. Why is the word "fun" in funeral!??? It's as if they're trying to say, "fun-for-all"!! Up until this time in my life I had only been to one other funeral. A friend of mine who I worked with, his little boy died unexpectedly. For those of you who have never been to a child's funeral, let me tell you, there is something so sad about a child's coffin. It is small, designed to fit an innocent little child. The impact of seeing that miniature coffin seemed to magnify the already unbearable sorrow of his shortened life.

For Mom's viewing Dad and my sisters decided on an open casket. I remember going through all the formalities of that day. It was then time for the family to go see/view the body. I walked up to the raised casket with half its lid up and looked down inside. It was probably the most haunting sight I'd ever been exposed to. It was like a bad horror movie. The inside of the coffin was beautifully decorated with fluffy pearl white silk made to look like a big soft pillow was ever-so-gently cuddling the person laying there. I say "the person", because someone who looked like my mom was in there. She was dressed in her best Sunday church dress. She had lots of makeup on. Mom was *not* a makeup person; I don't think she liked that looking down from Heaven. A blank, spiritless expression covered her face.

That's when I realized this would be the last memory I have of seeing her in person. I started cry. I quickly left the room.

My sisters tried to console me and then brought me back into the viewing room to see my mom again... "one last time", they said. I had to look at everything again; even though she was just a "thing" now. And that made me sob more.

The funeral was on February 7. That same day my dad's sister, Aunt Helen, died of an aneurysm (though she did not have

PKD). What!? I thought, "Does all this happen to everyone, or are we special for some reason!?"

Aunt Helen was an organ donor and directly and indirectly helped almost 40 people! My mom could not donate anything, which says a lot about the condition of her fragile body. RIP mom. RIP Aunt Helen.

PLEASE be an organ donor: www.organdonor.gov.

And if you already are a donor - THANK YOU! According to the American Transplant Foundation, as of 2018, there are 116,000 people in the United States waiting for a transplant, with another name added every ten minutes.

I always felt like I lost my mom when I was that nine year old little boy seeing her in the hospital after she had her stroke and she asked, "Who are you?".

I could not speak at her funeral.

Oh, I almost forgot: Do you think my mom's mom, my Baba/grandmother, came to her daughter's funeral? No. Do you think she called, sent a card, anything? No.

Friendship consists of a willing ear, an understanding heart and a helping hand.

~ Frank Tyger ~

Good Friends Are Everything

Another very good friend of mine got hired at a large investment firm. She kept telling me how great the company was. She even demonstrated to me this new technology called, "email". This was 1991, I was 25. She was able to electronically send a typed message to anyone in the company, and they could respond. Amazing!

And then, as if through divine intervention (and my Guardian Angel) it happened: the bank announced it was moving our center to San Francisco. I wasn't going north so I bought a nice suit for the interview at my friend's firm.

The interview lasted all day. I got the job. My career of everyday suit wearing in the financial industry had begun. Up until now I had no idea what I wanted to do, or be, when I 'grew up'. I was going to college for a Bachelor of Science (B.S.) degree in Business Management since that could help me in many different career paths. I didn't exactly know it at the time, but my life path was now set all by a change of events and some *very* special relationships - including my Guardian Angel, and my cross.

Notice every job I had, and would have in the future, was a result of a friendship I/we developed. Much the same for my dad and mom's lives, and probably for most people reading this. We are teaching our girls that friends – true friends – will help you in so many different ways and that being a great friend in return is the most rewarding feeling in the world.

My dad remarried to Sylvia on September 5, 1992. They had many things in common, including the fact that her husband was also very ill before he died. They knew of each other from Johnstown, PA. It was an interesting courtship as she lived in PA and Dad lived in CA. The relationship was hard for us Herman siblings to accept for a lot of reasons, especially after they moved back to PA. And to this day we have probably been too hard on, and not accepting enough, of Sylvia, who is a wonderful person.

Dad and Sylvia... and their paparazzi!

I studied, and passed, two securities exams while learning the investment business. The company had a full gym with showers so I was able to work out at lunch. The company often gave out great season tickets for the Los Angeles Dodgers. One time I took my sister's son, my nephew, Josh. We sat behind home plate on the third base side. The pitcher for the Dodgers came up to bat, a left handed batter.

Now every kid, every person's, dream when going to a baseball game is to catch a foul ball (or it should be!). So guess what happened? Josh was sitting on my lap. The batter hit a line drive foul ball to the left of me where no one was sitting. The ball bounced around and then started bouncing toward Josh and I. Just as the guy sitting in front of us reached back to grab the ball, I quickly reach down and snatched the ball instead.

I had it! My first - and only - precious foul ball. The Holy Grail was obtained!

The crowd started yelling, "Hold it up! Hold it up!" I gave the ball to my nephew (as any great uncle would), and he held it up. I remember a guy walking up the aisle stopped, and said, "He is never going to forget this!"

Well... Where is that special ball today? According to my sister, Josh played with the ball outside the next day. And, according to my sister, he then - lost - that priceless piece of history.

My job kept me busy learning a lot about the investing world. I was given the opportunity to travel to train new employees as we opened offices in various states. I was giving presentations all the time. I found traveling, with all expenses paid, and being single to be fun and rewarding!

I was now renting a room from some good friends, Gary and Yvonne. They are great people. We worked together, worked out together, carpooled together, played on the company's softball team together. It seemed we could never play enough softball. One game, I tried to dive back to first base after a hit. The first baseman came down hard on me, jamming my head into the rough infield sand. I got up a little dazed.

Someone then said my head was bleeding. I rinsed my head in the water fountain and went back to playing. When I got home I saw my head and it was literally - scalped! I had a 2 x 2 inch hole – my hair was gone and I was still bleeding.

I went to work the next day, not because I was tough, but to get a lot of attention! My manager sent me to the E.R. where they cleaned it out. If you're wondering, because I sure did wonder, yes, my hair did grow back!

I then accepted a job offer from a competitor and continued to work with financial advisors. We held conferences, which included 'wining & dining', and playing lots of golf with advisers regularly at the beautiful Pelican Hills Country Club in Newport Beach. If you're wondering how my scoliosis surgery and Harrington rod affected my playing, to this day I play golf but it is a little tough to get full hip and back rotation. But I have never used my scoliosis back as an excuse - for my bad playing!

I loved my job and I worked hard to not let anyone outwork me. I won various awards while working at the company, including a Tiffany's watch in 1997 - that I still have and proudly wear today, which is inscribed on the back, "MVP 1997". I was also "Employee of the *Company*" in 1998 out of a few hundred employees. My name is forever inscribed on a plaque on a wall somewhere.

I also came close to winning the award for most hours of volunteer work.

Another award, that my partner and I won, was a trip to the Skip Barber Dodge Driving School in Monterey, CA, at the beautiful Laguna Seca Raceway. They taught us professional driving skills, defensive moves, steering into a slide, and other cool moves. Then, we *raced* on their professional course in the famous Dodge Viper!

Since he and I were also responsible for sales in Northern California and Hawaii, I got to travel to Hawaii and "work". I remember him telling me not to wear a suit because everyone, including financial advisors, wears khakis and a Hawaiian shirt. Sweet! It was quite the experience traveling to Hawaii to work, particularly with all expenses paid, including more 'wining and dining' and golfing with our clients.

But despite the fun we would have, one trip I began suffering from a migraine. It built up throughout the day. I did not have any Tylenol and it got worse. We then took a client to dinner and all during our meal I had to keep getting up to go to the bathroom to try to get away from the noise and to put some cold water on my face. I even went outside thinking the fresh air may do some good. At the verge of collapsing from the tremendous pain, I finally told my coworker I had to leave. Thankfully, the client understood and she said she would say a prayer for me. As I got in the car I began to feel sick. I jumped out, moved to the front of the car where there was some grass and began throwing up.

It was during this time in my life that my migraines seemed to be getting worse, more frequent, and if possible more intense. Up until now I never thought to relate my migraines and PKD together. If I could get migraines to that intensity in Hawaii of all places, I needed answers.

So after a few more doctor appointments, and an ultrasound, I was *officially* diagnosed with Polycystic Kidney Disease. I remember asking the ultrasound technician if, "all those blacks things are cysts?" They were of course. I knew I probably had it anyway from my mom since the disease is hereditary. My two older sisters have it (more on them later). That began a new relationship with a nephrologist at age 30.

About a year later I experienced my first hernia. I was working out with my friend Jackson and felt a twinge of pain in my lower right side. I didn't think much of it but at at the end of a long work day my right groin area would always hurt. A few weeks later I finally went to the doctor and the next day I had reparative surgery. If you've never experienced a hernia, and yes, women can get them also, they are painful before, and after, the surgery. My surgeon informed me hernias are quite common in individuals with PKD due to weakening of the abdominal wall (45% have them).

The following year I had surgery to repair my meniscus (left knee). What was I doing you may ask when it tore? Weeding. Yes, that's right, weeding. I was stooped down and suddenly felt an incredible pain. The same excruciating pain I felt sitting with my legs behind me as a kid! But this time I could not get my leg to kick straight. It was stuck, bent at an almost 90 degree angle. It really hurt, but it scared me also.

Up until then I did not know what was the source of this unique pain. I thought it might be a muscle, which meant heat might relax the leg enough to straighten it. I hobbled from the front yard to the bathtub upstairs and took a very hot bath, soaking my leg while ever so slowly forcing my leg straight.

It was Sunday so I waited until the next day to go to my doctor. Now my leg was stuck straight. I could not bend it. (Yes, it was tough to drive.)

I remember sitting on the patient table and the doctor pushing down on my leg to try to get it to bend at the knee; it wouldn't and I was NOT keeping it straight. Now I was a little more scared. He said he was going to try to loosen it up with some type of medicine and the next thing I know he inserted a large needle into my knee joint. He waited a few minutes and started pushing again on my leg. Nothing. So, "let's try some more"... and another shot. Nothing, again.

The next day I went in for meniscus surgery. I woke with my knee wrapped up in elastic bandages and spent the next few weeks in physical therapy – which, anyone who has ever gone through knows, it's a lot of work.

The following year at age 32 I had hernia surgery - again. This time on my lower *left* side. As with the first hernia surgery, I was again warned that the painkillers would cause constipation if I wasn't careful. So I drank lots and lots of water while living in fear of having to strain to go #2. Not fun. I was beginning to understand just how serious this Polycystic Kidney Disease is, and all the secondary problems it was causing. But I was never going to give in! I just took whatever came at me in stride, and with a positive attitude.

And speaking of "never giving in", a good friend *dared* me to go skydiving with her. I was a little hesitant because of how the landing could impact my meniscus knee, scoliosis back with its Harrington rod, and still healing hernia. Oh yeah, and the fact you're jumping out of an airplane!

On October 18, 1997 we did the training, and then prepared to tandem (with a trainer) skydive over Lake Elsinore in CA. While I was in the plane I tried not to think about what was going to happen soon. If you let your mind go over everything that could go wrong, you would never do anything, let alone jump from a plane. Besides, I wanted to project confidence and that I was a real stud. Afterall, I was doing this in front of a lady friend.

My friend went first. I could not believe I just witnessed someone I knew jump out of the plane we were sitting in. I never thought she'd actually do it. I was going to do it, but I just thought she would chicken out. Now I HAD to do it!

It came to my turn. We crawled to the opening; lots of wind and cold. I tried not to look at the ground - 12,500 feet down! You are supposed to just fall and lay out flat but I dove, like into a pool, and we flipped! The next thing I know I'm free falling, floating. I was falling at 120 mph or 200 feet per second, but it felt like floating. I was supposed to pull the parachute cord at 5,000 feet but I was busy having fun and watching the camera guy filming this amazing experience; good thing the trainer was there. (The chute would have still been set-off automatically.) Once the canopy opened I was then instructed to pull down, left or right, depending on the way I wanted to turn and drop down.

During pre-training, they instruct you how to land: left your legs, let the instructor do the work, and slide-in on your bottom, which we did. I did almost lose my lunch after I landed because we did so many circle dives dropping-in to land. But, it was a phenomenal experience!

My migraines continued off and on. Now for those of you who have never had the fun experience of a migraine, please let me do my best to describe what it's like for me. First, usually there's a "trigger" - something that sets it off, but not always. For example, one of my triggers is not eating. I need to eat every so many hours or I get a migraine.

It starts with what feels a headache (though sometimes I wake up with a full blown migraine. More on this later). The pain intensifies and the drilling feeling begins in the right side of the head/temple. And then it gets worse. Now at this point, if I can take my Imitrex and rest I can usually knock it down and stop it. But sometimes the pain/drilling, loud noise, and any light begins to affect my psyche - and my stomach. I have to lay down in a dark room, close and cover my eyes, cover my ears, and try to not think about the pain – which is generally - impossible. The pain becomes prolonged and so intense that I can best describe it as a form of torture. An aura engulfs me causing vision issues and tingling in my hands and feet. I can't think straight. And after many hours of all that, I usually have to crawl to the bathroom to throw up all the medicines I may have taken earlier and then dry-heave. At that point I am a ball on the bathroom floor, literally crying, and praying to Jesus for help to end the pain.*

One of the websites I go to for more information is: www. migraines.com.

A man in love is incomplete until he is married. Then he is finished.

~ Zsa Zsa Gabor ~

(Guys, we can take this quote one of two ways.)

"Hello. You're In My Seat"

Until now I was doing *some* traveling as part of my job, but not full time. My friends and I always call being a Regional Vice President, "The greatest hidden job no one knows about." It is not on a job listing somewhere. You need to be inside the financial industry, and build a solid reputation. Sounds top secret, huh? And the joke was, no one ever could explain exactly what I did, and how I did it. I'm sure my family still can't.

Then, I got the call from an executive job recruiter. The company flew me to Chicago, picked me up in a town car. I interviewed the next day over lunch. I made sure to ask for the job and "close em". Always ask for the job when interviewing! I got the job! I was given a company car, a guaranteed minimum six figure salary (plus commissions), and they moved me to Northern California.

As my friends in the industry and I like to say, I was now "in the major leagues!" The territory I was responsible for was big: N Cal, OR, WA, HI, ID, MT, AK. Yes, there are HUGE moose often roaming the cities streets in Alaska! And the glaciers are breathtaking! My job was to increase sales by helping financial advisers sell our retirement products and life insurance to the general public. I created my own schedule, set my own appointments, created sales ideas and presentations, made my own flight/travel arrangements. I thrived being in a position of running my own company - but with the backing of a major corporation. Which is why one of my favorite movies is "Tommy Boy"; a hilarious look at life on the road!

It was on one of my first flights returning home from Seattle to Oakland after a long week when I met (my future wife) Linda. It was an Alaska Airlines plane with 3/2 seating - three seats on one side, two seats on the other. Someone was sleeping in her window seat so I, being the gentleman that I am, offered to have her sit next to me on the 2 seat side.

That began a conversation that determined we both had just started new jobs and requiring lots of traveling; we had just moved to Northern California; we lived 10 minutes from each other, and we didn't know anyone in the area! If this doesn't prove I have a Guardian Angel hard at work I don't know what would! When it came time to deplane I asked her for her number. She didn't give me her number, but she took my business card. I liked that.

Yes, she took a few long days to call. Our first date in the summer of 1999 was to the Pleasanton/Alameda County Fair. It was a fun day and then we went to an evening concert. It got dark and cold, and *someone* didn't bring a jacket, and I didn't wear one either. Linda was so cold; I felt so bad for her. We ended up leaving the show early. We first tried warming up in some of the exhibits buildings but that didn't work much. We finally made it to my car where I turned up the heat as high as it could go. The date ended with a quick kiss at her apartment door.

It was an amazingly fun courtship. Since we both traveled for our jobs we often happened to be in the same cities together, staying at great hotels, and eating at nice restaurants. Linda has a degree in medical imaging technology. She worked for

GE Healthcare as a clinical imaging specialist. Her job was to train x-ray technicians and surgeons on x-ray and imaging equipment.

Numerous times we were in Hawaii together; either I was working, or she was, or both! One time I was working in Fresno, CA, and Linda was in Hawaii for work. I was on my long drive home on a Thursday evening when unexpectedly my boss called. He said he needed me to cover and present at a conference in Hawaii! I got home, packed a bag, and jumped on a flight! Linda picked me up at the airport and we had a great time working, presenting, and playing in Hawaii. My Guardian Angel again!

I was in New York City, in the World Trade Center, in December, 2000, for a business conference I helped sponsor and host. We toured the NASDAQ, saw Wall Street, and the play "Chicago", among other entertaining hotspots. I ended the year 2000 – my first full year with the company and as an RVP - #1 in Sales!! I, the rookie, had beaten the veterans! The secret to my fast success - hard work, and making every effort to learn from the best. Every chance I got since before I started working I would ask someone successful how they do what they do. I would end 2001, #2 in Sales!

Then the impossible happened: I was in Fresno again on September 11, 2001 in my hotel getting ready for my day. I turned on the T.V. around 6:00 am pst. I saw a tall building on fire and wondered what country that was happening in. Once I realized it was New York City, and one of our beloved twin towers - where I was less than a year earlier - I called Linda and told her to turn on her T.V. Then we watched in horror as the second plane slammed into the second tower. We, and the world, were stunned.

I only learned both towers fell from some advisers I took to lunch that memorable day. I remember telling them, "No way! How!? That's impossible; those towers could never come down!"

Never Forget!

Then another, smaller, impossible happened: I was laid off that December, 2001. Merry Christmas! The company was closing their investment division and we were all let go. I called Linda in shock. She said, "Now what are we going to do!!" Wait, what!? How about lying and saying, "It's fine. We'll be okay." or "We can handle this.", or "I love you poopsy.", etc. I had to tell *her...* it would be ok! And this was going to be my future wife!???

As if my blood pressure wasn't high enough due to my enlarging PKD kidneys, being unemployed was so hard, as I know many of you can relate. I could not sleep. Every single second of the day I stressed about how and where I could find a job. I never thought about unemployment benefits – I was determined not to take any assistance just like previous Herman generations.

Linda had always wanted to move back home near her parents in Oregon where she grew up so we decided to move. I was familiar with the Oregon/Washington border area because of my client friends there. I was 37, unemployed, and moving to a new state.

Sounds like the pioneering path my parents took when they were just starting out.

In February, 2002, I had my first good job prospect. I flew to Seattle and met my future boss in a hotel conference room for an interview. Picture this with me: as I walked into the room he had arranged a number of large tables into a big square. The square was probably forty feet by forty feet in diameter. He was sitting at the far end of the tables and the only other chair was located at the opposite end of the tables near the door I just walked through. Instinctually, I grabbed the chair and brought it all the way over next to where he was sitting while asking him, "Do you mind if I move next to you?" After a few simple questions, the interview was over.

Leaving the hotel and on the flight home, I couldn't help but wonder if I was going to be offered the job since the interview was so short, and different. I did ask for the job before I left but he was vague. Two days later, I was offered and accepted the Regional Vice President position covering the same five Pacific Northwest states I had at my previous employer.

Since I now had a job Linda agreed to marry me!

We were married on August 3, 2002, in Vancouver, WA, at the historic Academy, which was once a Catholic school for girls, built in 1871. It has the most beautiful church/wedding chapel. The area is the historical Fort Vancouver and Officers Row. (Also think, Lewis and Clark, because they traveled here along the Columbia River on their historic expedition.) Our reception and dinner were held at The (Ulysses S.) Grant House built in 1849. We traveled from the church to the reception in a horse-drawn, blue carriage. It was beautiful!! You should have been there!

We bought a house. We put in most of the landscape by ourselves. Linda's dad – with his tractor - and her brother Gary, helped a lot. But my work/traveling and working on the landscaping became more difficult as my strength was fading. I was also anemic but I didn't know it. I blamed myself for not being in better shape, for not working out/exercising enough. I was exhausted all the time though not wanting to admit it was from the effects of my Polycystic Kidney Disease. And I did not want anyone to worry, especially Linda.

Rob, Gary, and Dad – on his tractor in back.

Then one time while I was being prepped to donate blood, the nurse pricked my finger, tested the blood drop, and then asked, "Do you know you're anemic?" I said, "No... but does that make you tired?" My days of donating blood were over. I would soon thereafter begin receiving regularly scheduled EPO, or erythropoietin, injections. EPO reduces fatigue by increasing production of the bodies red cells and increasing oxygen absorption.

PKD was slowly affecting my overall quality of life more than I chose to admit. Linda and I became involved with the PKD Foundation fund-raising efforts, chapter meetings, and annual walks. We gift wrapped books at a bookstore, raised money from local businesses, friends donated money, and my employer matched any of my contributions. I even combined my work with philanthropic work by sponsoring advertising for my advisors businesses that also benefited the PKD Foundation. It was a win for everyone involved.

Portland, OR Walk for PKD!

Dr. Julie Tank, Internal Medicine, Nephrology, at Northwest Renal Clinic in Portland, OR, became my #1 doctor in January of 2004. She is a phenomenal nephrologist and I don't know where my health condition would be without her. Dr. Tank received her doctoral degree from Oregon Health Sciences University in Portland, OR. She a Medical Director for Fresenius Kidney Care Home Dialysis, she is also on the Medical Advisory Board for Fresenius Kidney Care. Her Society membership list is distinguished and too long to list here.

One time as we were concluding an office visit where I felt like a truck had just hit me, I asked Dr. Tank if I could give her a hug because she has been such a huge help to me over the years. I think I shocked her with the request but I stole a hug anyway!

My favorite nephrologist, Dr. Tank.

Blessed be childhood, which brings down something
of heaven into the midst of our rough earthliness.

~ Henri Frederic Amiel ~

KK!

When Linda became pregnant the summer of 2004 we were thrilled! I knew Linda wanted children. Some people may ask why we chose to have a child with the increased risk of passing on my PKD. I hear you, because I asked the very same question of my dad when I was diagnosed with the horrible disease. At the time he just looked at me but didn't even have to answer. What I was really asking of course was, "Would I have rather not been born at all?" I never again thought of "not being born", as a way to defeat a disease.

Then in October my sister, Laura called saying my sister, Jan, was in the hospital. She had suffered a cerebral hemorrhage from PKD - just like my grandfather and my mom – though not nearly as severe. She would be fine. What's even more astounding is that it happened thirty years after – almost to the very day – of my mom's devastating hemorrhage in October of 1974.

Linda, now in full pregnancy, retired in January, 2005, from her very successful imaging career. One of our Hawaii trips was an all-expenses-paid award trip for Linda.

Our first child, Kaley Shea Herman, was born on Sunday night, March 20, 2005. She was healthy. She did have a full head of hair and did not like to sleep or to take to feeding. She did like to cry - all the time. It was extremely frustrating and exhausting for us. Linda and I were already dealing with my worsening health. And Linda was using breast pumps, and tubes, and almost anything to feed this child. And someone at the hospital told us to make sure the baby ate every few hours. We found out the hard way, that was *the worst advice ever*! Never, NEVER, ever wake a sleeping baby – for ANY reason – if you like sleep! And your sanity!

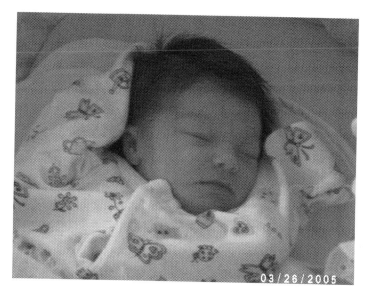

Of course, from day one with Kaley we were concerned about Polycystic Kidney Disease. ADPKD = Autosomal Dominant PKD is typically the "adult" version. Since ADPKD runs in my family's genetic code, we knew Kaley would be at risk for this "adult" version much later in her life (or so we thought).

I was back to traveling the next week, which, in hindsight was one of the dumbest thing I ever did – not being there more with Linda and "KK", as Linda recovered during that tough time.

By the way, "KK" is a nickname I came up with one day for Kaley and we've used it ever since. Sorry, there is no special meaning behind it; it's just catchy! Don't you think?

Flying was/is never fun: late flights, canceled flights, missed flights, rude fellow travelers, rude flight attendants, lost luggage, the weather issues, etc. And flying into Juneau, AK requires a maneuver only a few pilots are trained for because of the mountains. The plane flies in very low and then make a 90 degree left turn down onto the runway. They actually make an announcement before the drop to warn passengers. It was crazy the first time, and every time, I experienced it.

And covering ID, MT, and AK – I encountered weather issues. Yes, I traveled to AK in the 'dread' of winter. Sometimes my rental car wouldn't start in the morning. Or dealing with the reality of my outside temperature dash gauge showing -10 degrees. How'd you like to work in that in a nice suit? (Yes, they wear suits in Alaska.)

But the worst weather I often encountered was not in Alaska, but in Montana believe it or not. My regular travel routine was to fly into Billings on a Sunday (there was only one flight from Portland to Montana daily at 2:30pm), to start my week. After two business days in Billings, I would then drive west at night to Bozeman, visit clients there, drive at night north to Great Falls, spent one day there, then at night drive southwest to Missoula, work and then fly home. I did this routine in Montana every 6 or 7 weeks for years.

The driving was always interesting in my territory just due to animals on the roads and Montana was no exception. So take an 80 mph speed limit, nighttime, animals, bad drivers – especially some truckers, my exhaustion, and add in a nasty blizzard, and all that equals white-knuckle driving while in a suit. The long blizzard drives were so bad sometimes I made a plan with Linda to call her every so many miles and tell her where I was and if I didn't call her she was to call the Highway Patrol. Thank you God for cell phones.

Through more hard work, I ended 2005 in the Top 8 in Sales, and qualified for our Advisory Board. I ended 2006 in the Top 8 in Sales, and again qualified for the Advisory Board all despite my continuing and worsening health issues. In fact, some of you can probably relate to this: most of my co-workers thought I was anti-social because I was always the first person to leave an evening event and head back to my hotel room to relax and sleep. In fairness most of them probably didn't know I was ill. But the ones who did know often seemed to imply or say, "You don't look sick", or "You seem fine." Oh... thanks???

My nephrologist, Dr. Julie Tank – did I mention the best doctor ever! - had tracked my kidney failure date to the end of 2008/ beginning 2009. She had charted out the declining progression as things got worse and worse. I was placed on the kidney transplant list in 2006 at age 41. Working was getting tougher especially since I always had to be on my "A" game while building relationships and selling. I was also still traveling 95% of the time.

During the summer of 2006 we discovered Linda was *finally* pregnant again. Our many prayers were answered! Kaley would now have a brother or sister. The three of us playfully debated whether a boy or a girl would fit better into our growing family. Of course, I wanted a little boy while Linda and Kaley wanted another little girl. Linda had an early ultrasound at 7 weeks and the heart rate was fine. At 10 weeks she went in for her first prenatal appointment and the doctor couldn't hear a heartbeat. They had her go to the hospital where they confirmed with ultrasound - she no longer had a viable pregnancy.

Our biggest nightmare had come true; Linda would a few weeks later have a D&C - a surgery sometimes necessary when you don't miscarry.

For me, and most certainly for Linda, this would be the saddest, most heartbreaking thing to have to deal with.* I can only imagine the pain Linda went through and probably still goes through when she thinks about that precious little baby. Another piece of my heart was gone. The 'what could have been' is still too much to think about. But Jesus would once again have a different plan for our family's ongoing "tornado".

I buried myself back into work.

With regards to work, I always understood I was not the best salesperson, or presenter, or certainly not the healthiest, or the person with the best personality, and I was not the best *natural* RVP. But I did know I could be the hardest working employee and no one can beat that. I want to be the best example for my kids and I teach them hard work will triumph over any lack in abilities all of us have. But the competitor in me also knew that time was not on my side as my energy dragged. And that pushed me to try to work even harder.

But I didn't tell many people I met with while working that I was sick but often it was too difficult to hide. One time I was at lunch in Bellevue, WA with two advisors/friends when one of them unexpectedly reached across the booth table and grabbed my hands. They knew I was, and am, a Christian so I thought he wanted to pray with me - something I often did with clients. Instead, he held my hands and asked me, "Rob, why are you always shaking so much?" It completely caught me off guard. I wondered if I should tell him the truth or make up some excuse. I told them the truth about my kidney disease. They immediately prayed for me right there at the table. It strengthened our relationships more than I thought possible.

Another time I was at an advisor's home in Boise, ID meeting with her in her living room. My meds often gave me a very dry mouth making it difficult to talk; I kept licking my lips. I was so embarrassed. She kept offering me water but my pride, and not wanting to tell her I was ill, lead me to politely respond, "No thank you." I probably should have told her, but I hesitated because it was our first meeting. Looking back it would have been a great opportunity to educate someone about PKD. She never did any business with me.

I even had my competitors trying to use my health against me once word got out – telling advisors, "You don't want to do business with Rob. He's sick."

My busy schedule often had me up at 3:00 a.m. on a Monday to catch a 6:00 a.m. flight somewhere, then work all day and often late into the evening. I remember one trip coming back from MT when I was very sick – throwing up, dizziness, heavy sweating, chills, fever, etc. To get from Great Falls, MT back to Portland, I had to fly through Seattle first - nothing direct. I did *not* want to miss my flights, or spend time in a Great Falls Emergency Room. I was so miserable on those flights. I wondered how much more I could take.

But I never gave up; never gave in. And in 2007, I qualified #1 in sales!

As I mentioned earlier, I/we like doing our own landscaping – it is great exercise - outdoors and gives a sense of pride and accomplishment. It also keeps me motivated, and like my job, it kept my mind off my PKD condition. Linda and I purchased a large play structure for Kaley in early 2008 and despite my worsening health issues I was determined to put this thing together with help from (Linda's) Dad – Lester Troyer.

The proud papa in me couldn't wait to see my precious KK and her little friends playing on it. Our backyard corner was unevenly sloped grass so we first needed to first build a raised, level base, with supports on which the structure would stand. Then we followed the instructions, page by numerous page for the structure, trying to stay dry from rain and snow. We then stained it, and after about 8 days, our work-of-art was complete! I could not have completed this project without all of Dad's help. (And it still looks great to this day, though when we sold the house we regrettably had to leave it behind.)

The time finally came halfway through 2008 when I was no longer able to travel for my job. The company allowed me to work from home because I was physically and mentally exhausted and moving up on the transplant list. I know many people lose their jobs due to heartless employers looking out for their bottom line instead of good employees; that is so wrong! During my career, at least to this point, all of my employers – some of the biggest companies in the world - took very good care of me while understanding my needs for time off for doctor appointments, being sick, etc.

2008 was also the year of the Great Recession, but I ended the year being #1 in sales again! In fact, it was the best year of my career despite constant fatigue and no longer traveling or meeting with my clients face-to-face for half the year. I had great clients!

Now each year in January we all traveled to Dallas, TX to celebrate the previous year's successes and plan for the new year's expectations and goals. It was always exciting, and extremely humbling, to have your professional colleagues give your efforts recognition with an award, and an ovation.

In early January, 2009, my bosses sent *a video company* to our home to film my award acceptance speech because I couldn't travel due to my health. (Did I have the best managers? Yes!)

Kaley was four years old and I wanted her in the video. It was emotionally difficult to speak about the previous year's sales efforts, my health, and why I couldn't be there with them. Somehow they were able to piece together enough tape between all my leaking eyes and sniffling. The next day my manager called to tell me the over 500 fellow co-workers, and their family members gave me a standing ovation after they watched my video at our annual National Sales Meeting! I still have that video; it is an enormous sense of pride for me.

My kidneys were now functioning at just 10%, and it felt at times that my entire body was too.

On December 27, 2008 I also started a journal on www. caringbridge.org to inform family and friends of my day-to-day progress. The following are exact excerpts, or paraphrases of excerpts:

"I had surgery on January 8, 2009, to create a fistula in my left arm for dialysis, but they did not want to touch the hernia I had developed on my right side - again. It was an all day outpatient surgery, meaning I was home the same day I went in. When I woke, I had a 2 inch incision taped up at the top inside of my left forearm just at the crease where my arm bends. My doctor said my veins were "spasming" during the attachment, but everything went well."

"My arm was very sore and Oxycodone was my friend for a few days following my surgery. I was instructed to relax and keep my arm elevated. I did neither as I (always) had a lot of work to get done; my life story. My doctor told me the burning feeling was caused by cutting through the nerves."

"After a fews weeks it had grown to its "attractive" state. I always thought my fistula was 'pretty - pretty unique', meaning *pretty ugly*. Of course, I could feel the blood rushing through it but I could also *hear* it. That took some getting used to. Weird!"

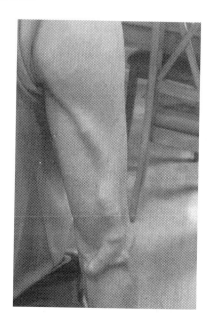

January 24, 2009, Linda wrote: "Rob spent most most of the night last night in the bathroom sick. We think it's the flu, he aches all over, has a temperature of 101 degrees, and is very cold. He hasn't been able to eat much today or keep down much."

January 25: "We got "The (kidney transplant) Call" this morning at 4:45am! We had to turn it down due to my flu."

February 18, 3:08 am!: "I have been up for an hour now laying in bed. My sleep patterns are so erratic, it drives me nuts! I am always tired, but I can't sleep at night and want to sleep during the day."

March 2: "The DJIA hits a 12 year low to 6763! My diet is to limit protein, sodium, potassium, and phosphorus. Ever read a food label??? I think grass is the only thing that doesn't contain these ingredients! I've lost 20 lbs; not good. It's been six weeks since "The Call."

My dialysis began in March, 2009. I was 44. After arriving at my center, I was given the basic instructions and then weighed in. I washed my fistula area very good. You, and they, want this area germ-free. When I went inside I was deeply saddened to see so many of our military veteran heroes there going through dialysis. It was very quite, sad, and depressing.

I brought a pillow, a blanket, warm clothes – I cut the left sleeve off of my sweatshirt, a book to read, and my work laptop. The nurse took my blood pressure standing, and sitting, and then all my other vitals. Once I settled in the nurse asked if I wanted numbing medicine. Trying to be tough I told him I didn't need it. But I was nervous. He seemed concerned.

The nurse said, "Okay then, here we go", and proceeded to stick one big 16 gauge needle in (the average blood draw uses a 21 gauge). It faced north, in my left arm/fistula near my lower bicep. Then #2 needle goes in above, facing south. Or so he tried. It immediately infiltrated. He stops the bleeding externally and tries poke #3 higher up. Same result, and now my arm is on fire, burning from the pain, and bleeding internally.

The next thing I know there was a group of nurses around me, with two literally playing rock-paper-scissors to determine who pokes next. Someone loses and needle #4 goes in (needle #1 still in.) Apparently it takes and we begin filtering. Yea!?

But then for some reason, a nurse fittles with the needle they just put in and = problem! More pain, more fire. After about an hour or so of all this the head nurse determines enough is enough. They pull the needles. Go home. We'll try again next week.

Dialysis day #2. My arm is beginning to turn black and blue. But this time no problem for my nurse to get the needles in. He tells me the goal is to get me to 14 gauge needles. Yea again!

I went to dialysis twice a week, six hours each session. Each time they had problems with my arm/fistula infiltrating – bleeding internally. I sat in a big chair. I tried to work. I read "Lone Survivor", by Navy Seal Marcus Luttrell. (There's a guy who Never Gave in!) You also can't move for six hours except to go to the bathroom and then they have to unhook you.

The nurses are supposed to constantly monitor everything because of things that could go wrong, particularly cramping muscles. One time, I started to cramp up in my right thigh. I called for help. No one came. It got worse and worse – tighter and tighter – until I thought my leg muscle was *literally* going to rip off the bone. It was horrible! Remember, I couldn't even stand up because I was hooked up in the chair. I was completely defenseless. I screamed some bad words. Someone finally adjusted the machine, and the pain/cramping stopped.

Due to the infiltrating eventually my arm swelled to two times bigger and turned black, blue, and purple. I was exhausted when finished with a session but I also couldn't wait to stand up and stretch. Besides any cramping, the worst part was having to press on my arm to stop the bleeding when they took the needles out. Just like when you get blood work done, you must put pressure on the needle opening to stop any potential bleeding afterwards. Now imagine your worst bruise and having to push on it - hard. And that bruise has two big holes from the needles they just pulled out of you.

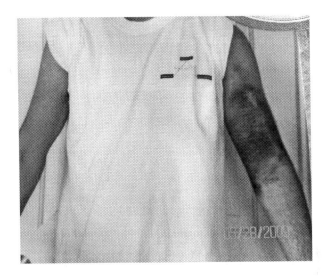

Many times while I was standing after completing my dialysis session I was so tired, and because of the pain, I couldn't put enough pressure on my arm to stop the bleeding. Someone eventually would say, "Hey man, you're doing it again.", meaning there was now blood on the floor. I would then have to put pressure back on my arm again as someone cleaned up the floor.

Blessed are those who can give without remembering, and take without forgetting.

~ Elizabeth Bibesco ~

"We Have A Kidney For You!"

It had been almost two years since getting on the kidney transplant list. We looked into various cities and states as a way to shorten my wait time. Yes, you can go anywhere and transfer your wait time already accrued. You just have to be available when they call, and also be available for follow up clinic appointments.

Because of my renal diet I couldn't eat anything but "grass" – I used to joke. Because of my restricted diet I did lose weight. Not that I needed to; I was 6' 2" and now weighed only 155 lbs.

I received two calls about 8 weeks apart from my doctors stating they had a kidney for me. The first time was on January 25 but I had the flu. The second came on April 1 at 11:30 pm, but the person had TB in the last 10 years so my doctors thought it would be too risky considering my health issues.

Linda and I had many philosophical and ethical discussions on what if the person donating was not a good person. (Is that "normal", or do I have yet another issue I need to deal with???)

After having continuing frustration with the first dialysis center, I switched to a new dialysis center. My new nurse was getting me ready for my session and Linda was leaving after saying goodbye as usual. It was a beautiful Saturday morning, April 4, 2009. I was 44.

Suddenly, Linda and Kaley came running back in saying they had a message that stated my doctors had a good kidney for me! They were so excited! I was so excited! The people at dialysis were happy for me! I no longer had the flu! And the best part, I wouldn't have to do one more dialysis session Good Lord willing - ever! I was getting a new kidney!! And a new life!!

I jumped out of that chair and we left the center. We were almost home to get everything ready when in talking with the coordinator and doctors, they wanted me to do one more dialysis session. I tried to talk them out of it but they wanted my blood as clean as possible, just in case. They also informed me they were transplanting one of the deceased donor kidneys into another patient. My operation would come later that night.

So we drove back to the dialysis center, plunged in the two needles and sat back for a quick four hour cleaning. As I sat there I tried not to let people notice as I began to cry. So many things flew through my head, so many prayers answered. I also remembered that my mom never got a chance to experience this joyous feeling. I said a prayer to her.

Excited and a little nervous, Linda and I checked into Good Samaritan hospital that Saturday evening around 4:00pm. Next came blood work, an I.V., an EKG, a chest x-ray, and different people coming in at different times all telling us what they were all responsible for during this production. The waiting game was tough. They finally came in around 8:30 pm, and said they were ready for me. Linda and I said our goodbyes. We told each other it would be okay and that we loved each other. I went in for my surgery around 9:00 pm. I was tired, but anxious.

Now anytime I've had surgery I have always tried to stay awake as long as possible when they wheeled me into the operating room. I wanted to try to take in and remember as much as possible. The rooms are always very brightly lit, cold, with plenty of chrome and steel everywhere. There are lots of people talking to each other, and to me - telling me to slide over to the operating table, what this or that was for, how long it would take, etc. And then the anesthesiologist says he or she is going to give me some medicine through my I.V. to make me "sleepy". By that point, it's really tough to force my eyes to stay open. Then a mask is placed over my nose and mouth and I'm told to take some deep breaths.

Also, I always ask the surgeon and nurses anytime I am having surgery to have someone take a picture of whatever they were removing, repairing, etc. (Is that too weird???) For this surgery I was given a great picture of my new kidney going in. (Please see the photo in the last chapter, titled: "Area 51")

I was kidney transplant #724 for Legacy Good Samaritan, NW Transplant Services, in Portland, OR, headed by the famous Dr. William Bennett, M.D., MACP (Master of American College of Physicians). Dr. Bennett was the first person awarded a research grant, for $25,000.00, by the

PKD Foundation (www.pkdcure.org). He was later awarded the PKD Foundation Jared J. Grantham Distinguished Achievement Award.

I had 16 staples for a 16 inch incision that ran from my right side curving down to the top of my private area. The catheter and all the drains and tubes were not fun, particularly the PICC line in my neck. A PICC line is a peripherally inserted central catheter which makes for ease of administering medicines. Unlike an I.V., it does not need to be changed every so many days which makes it much more convenient for the patient, and nurses.

I was told my kidney came from a deceased 22 year old female. THANK YOU to her and her family for making the brave, selfless decision to be an organ donor.

Again, PLEASE be an organ donor, and encourage others to be!

I was released from the hospital on April 10 - GOOD FRIDAY! And I believe that was NO coincidence. I was home in time to spend Easter with my family all because of the heroic decision of my organ donor. Thank you JESUS.

For the first few weeks I had regular transplant clinic visits. My left arm - my dialysis arm - was my biggest challenge. It was still bruised black and blue and purple. At times the arm pain and burning was more than I thought I could handle. I asked every doctor and nurse I could about my arm and if there was anything they could recommend to heal it. They all said the same thing, "Give it time.", and once again, that infamous line, "Don't worry."

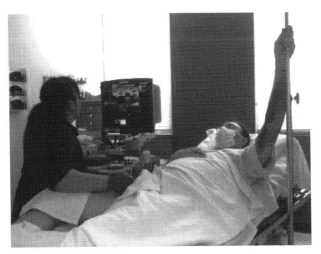

Rob's ultrasound, his bruised left arm
due to infiltrating from dialysis.

During my time on dialysis and in the hospital our 4 year old Kaley had a tough time with all the sitters and time away from her mom and dad. She also probably didn't like seeing her dad in the shape I was in lately. She fought through it, and when she would say, "Daddy, I am sorry you are not feeling good." or "Are you feeling better today Daddy?" it melted my heart.

My numbers continued to improve while the side effects from all the medications also continued: headaches, shakiness, dizziness, and then swelling started in my right leg and foot. They did an ultrasound to check for blood clots but everything was clear. I also met the recipient of the other kidney from the donor. A great guy named Jim, who was well deserving and needing of his gift of life.

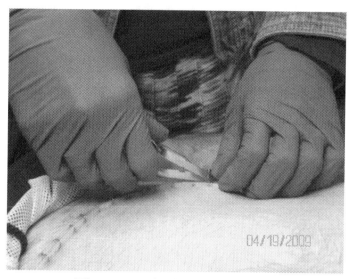

The 16 staples being removed.

During this timeframe the swine flu broke out. It was a big concern for those of us who had transplants and/or were on immune suppression drugs. So no shaking hands, including at church. And for a while I wore a protective breathing mask.

I noted in my journal doctors being concerned it was taking so long for the swelling, and black, blue, and purple, to heal in my left arm.

May 4th was one month!

Here's my journal entry for May 5th :

"I woke with my typical headache and by 11:00am, I was throwing up. The pain in my head was very intense, worse than my typical migraine. I got sick five more times. I had hot and cold flashes, and could not keep water down. Linda called Dr. Bennett and the next thing I know the paramedics are at our house. Dr. Bennett wanted fluids and pain meds in me as soon as possible. Of course, it took three tries to get in the I.V. in while in the ambulance. I then apparently kept asking for more morphine."

Due to our family history of aneurysms there was concern this could be the cause. I had blood work and a CT, then a night being watched in the hospital. I agreed with Dr. Bennett and Linda that if I was not feeling better by morning they could perform a spinal tap. (How would that work with a Harrington rod attached to my spine from the scoliosis? Thank you Jesus I never had to find out.) I was never told what the cause of this illness was.

May 12th I wrote this funny story: "My first trip out in public was to the grocery store with my sister. Because of my incision it was difficult to wear pants at the normal hip level; because of this I wore my sweat pants pulled very high up. I had also tucked in my shirt so it was not a good look. Then add my glasses, a baseball cap, and due to my surgery, I was walking funny. Can you visualize my look? Yikes! Flashbacks to my freshman year!

I went to the restroom and when I came out I was looking very confused and lost trying to find my sister. I started noticing various looks and stares but I thought it was because somehow people knew I just had a kidney transplant.

As we were leaving any employee who saw me was staring and waving and saying, "Goodbye" and/or "bye bye", and "Have a nice day", but in a slower, extra nice and sensitive way. I was thinking, 'How do these people know I had a transplant?'

It wasn't until I got in the car that it dawned on me the reason everyone was being so nice was because my pants were pulled way up, shirt tucked in, glasses, baseball hat, funny walk, and then looking lost. They thought I was a person with special needs... and I started cracking up!

Laughter is truly the best medicine!!" (No, I don't have a picture... and I'm glad I don't!)

June 2nd I had my first required biopsy. I brought along Linda and Kaley. After the ultrasound my doctor, Dr. Batiuk, figures where and at what angle (32 degrees) the biopsy tool will go in. Two shots of novocaine into my incision did not feel good. Then he sticks the tool/needle inside me to take a kidney sample, then one "click", then another "click".

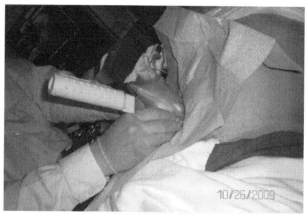

My new kidney gets a biopsy from Dr. Batiuk.

The next day I was told the kidney looked great and is working fine.

While I was out of work for about the next 3 months time was spent walking, eating right to regain the weight, drinking lots and lots of water, and rebuilding my strength and stamina. I will be on various anti-rejection medicines for the rest of my life (based on current protocol). It took *many* months and a lot of trial and error for all of us to figure out the correct combination of transplant and immune suppression medicines. This doesn't get talked about a lot but for me it was often frustrating and difficult dealing with all the various side effects of medications, and combinations of medications. So if you are going through this, or have gone through that, I can absolutely relate.

Note: All the medicines turned my once brown hair – to black! (But in case you are wondering, my eyes are still brown.) My medications also affected the skin on my forehead. To this day, I have a peculiar line which separates my normal tan-ish skin, with white, pale looking skin from the line up to my hairline.

Part of my rehab included my participation in a National Institute of Health study on B cell antibodies. I tested positive for some antibodies so I received several infusions of a drug called Rituximab. Being part of the study was another blessing in my life because the study discovered – early – that my body was going through a bout of kidney rejection prior to many of the normal symptoms showing. After various tunings and adjustments, my doctors - thankfully – were able to stop the rejection.

Nothing can stop the man with the right mental attitude from achieving his goal; nothing on earth can help the man with the wrong mental attitude.

~ W. W. Ziege ~

This Can't Be Happening

The three months went by and I slowly went back to work on the "road" the week of July 17, 2009, traveling to Seattle, presenting, and building my sales back up. It of course took time to build up my stamina but it felt good to be productive again. I did have my days of not feeling well. On one particular day after a few meetings in one of Seattle's tallest skyscrapers, I was suffering from a migraine and feeling worn out. I made it down to my car in the underground parking garage, attempting to rest. The next thing I knew I was throwing up in the garage from the pain.

Almost a year to the day of my kidney transplant our family participated in the "Threads for Life" quilt making event presented by Donate Life Northwest. (www.donatelifenw.org) Linda's sister-in-law Jeanne made a beautiful quilt square to celebrate my kidney transplant from a deceased donor on April 4, 2009. Her square was then sewn into a guilt containing other transplant donors and/or recipients squares. The handmade-with-love quilt was then hung on display in Salem, OR, and around the state. If you ever have the opportunity to participate in this type of event, or any event celebrating kidney donors and recipients, please do so; they are very humbling, and you meet some great people!

The Organ Donor quilt, and Linda,
Kaley, Rob, Grandma, Grandpa.

Prior to and during my recovery Kaley was experiencing headaches every so often. We didn't think much of it and she wasn't one to complain about things. She was just 5 years old and still having headaches. But now they seemed to be happening more often, with more intensity. So Linda made an appointment with her doctor. I was praying KK didn't inherit my migraines, or my Polycystic Kidney Disease.

The pediatrician said to keep a journal and come back in two weeks. We did so. She then ordered an MRI to be done at Oregon Health and Science University (OHSU). Kaley went in for an MRI on August 20, 2010. They sedated her for the test. They then sent her home. A few hours later we received a call from her pediatrician asking us to take her to the ER, where the pediatric neurosurgeon would meet us. What!? The doctor said she had a *brain cyst*. What!!? It was large, 4cm, and it was compressing her cerebellum and displacing part of her brain. We sat in the ER all evening waiting for a room. They were going to admit her to do some more tests; it was a Friday night.

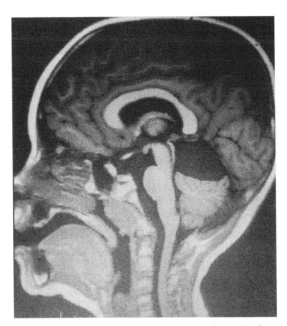

Kaley's cyst - the large black spot to the right below her brain.

Linda went home and I stayed with Kaley - still waiting. We finally got a room at 2am! They decided to put an IV in. They had a terrible time and so did Kaley. I had to hold Kaley down as she screamed. After numerous attempts by a male nurse, I finally said, "Come on, man!" That did *not* help the situation.

After an eye exam, another MRI with contrast, and meeting with the neurosurgeon, the plan was to go home and come back in two weeks for surgery to relieve the pressure in the cyst. They can not remove it. It is part of her brain, but draining it would help.

On Sept. 20, 2010 we got up at 4am and drove Kaley to Doernbecher Children's Hospital in Portland, OR. Linda researched the surgery, the surgeons, and all possible solutions, even requesting they use surgical navigation, a computer assisted technology. The surgeon said he didn't think he needed it but changed his mind the night before so Kaley had to have yet another CT the morning before surgery. Knowing the surgeon would soon be using a bone saw to remove part of her skull was nearly unbearable.

The surgery was long, recovery was scary. Kaley was very nauseated for days - and we kept worrying something went wrong. They reassured us this was common after brain surgery. They put her very long hair up on top of her head, and the incision was about four inches long at the base of her skull. Ironically, the pile of her long, thick hair was on her head for so many days that it became one giant tangled, dread lock, and sadly had to be cut out.

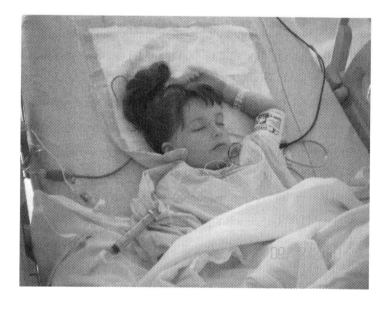

Kaley handled everything with maturity beyond her five years keeping a positive attitude throughout. She "Never Give In". She still has the cyst, it remains stable and is 1-2 cm. Her symptoms are better but she still gets occasional headaches and gets extremely car sick any time we drive for any distance.

It was extremely tough to see Kaley have to go through that experience, and it was also just as tough to see all the other children in that hospital going through their own challenges.

Maybe it was part of God's plan for me to see the other suffering children to help put so many of my lifelong personal things in perspective. It was spiritually humbling. God Bless those kids, their parents, and all the great hospital staff!

One small bright note: The day before Kaley's surgery a lady delivered to our house a new bike for her. I had entered her name in a drawing while we were at the Vancouver, WA Fair over the summer... and she won!

One side note: A number of my clients and I did a number of fundraising, charity golf events to benefit Doernbecher Children's Hospital, never thinking that one day my child might need their incredible services.

The next month in October my dad's brother, my favorite uncle, Uncle Joe, died. Our family spent a lot of time at their home on the lake in Pennsylvania while growing up. The three of us flew out to New York for a few days in New York City and then went on to his military funeral. It was a beautiful tribute. Thankfully, Kaley had no problems flying being so close to her surgery and recovery. RIP Uncle Joe.

The Herman family's life plans would change yet again. The company I was working for had some financial problems during the two year recession. So once again, I was... laid off. And once again, right before Christmas.

We stopped asking, "What else?", because "what else" was always right around the corner. With my, and Kaley's, ongoing healthcare costs, a mortgage, and other financial responsibilities I once again was unable to relax. During the Christmas season I tried to focus on what was important - my family, and all our many blessing.

January, 2011 seemed to take forever to get through with no good job prospects and a whole lot more stress. There were so many times when I felt so alone just trying to cope with the magnitude of the present. And there was no way I was going to let Linda see anything but strength. I knew she was also being pushed to her breaking point; *we* as a couple were being pushed to our breaking point.

February came and lots more prayers brought me an interview. I accepted the offer and flew to Cincinnati, OH for training and then another trip to the headquarters in Birmingham, AL. Until now I had worked with the most amazing, nicest, people in my life in this industry – the financial and/or investments, industry. But my new manager was not a nice person. Not to boast but I had been in the industry for over fifteen years and was in the top quartile for most of my career to that point.

I contacted Human Resources. I was told I was not in a "protected class". There was nothing they would do. I contemplated my options as I, for the first time in my career, I actually *hated* going to work. I was physically unhealthy, and mentally depressed.

But my Guardian Angel would be watching out for me again. My former boss and mentor, Bill Lowe, called me that November saying he was starting a new company. He wanted me to cover the Pacific Northwest again. So I called my current manager and very professionally told him I was resigning. I'll leave it up to your imagination regarding what I *wanted* to say...

A child is a person who is going to carry on what you have started... the fate of humanity is in her hands.

~ Abraham Lincoln ~

Our Journey!

Since the birth of our now beautiful Kaley and devastating "miscarriage" five years later we had been trying desperately to have another child. But my PKD was not helping our efforts. When everything - including in-vitro fertilization with Linda giving herself shots in the stomach - failed, we decided to become foster parents for the state of Washington. It also meant a lot for us to be able to give back while helping some great kids. We went through the required classes in the evening for a few weeks, interviewed, and took our required first aid course on a Saturday.

Please go to www.adoptuskids.org for more information on becoming a foster parent.

The experience will change you for the better and you will absolutely change a child's life for the better. These precious kids need someone to just love them.

One thing I didn't mention earlier: Do you remember our friend Chuck from our growing up days? He was the one I slid down the mountain with. Well, his dad was single and was a foster parent to Chuck and two other kids. Chuck might not have grown up in a rich, two parent family, but he sure felt loved!

Also my sister, Laura and her husband Don are adoptive parents to their two now grown boys - James and Eric.

We fostered a number of beautiful babies and kids and we wanted to save them all. (We also fostered a momma cat and her kittens. Adorable!! And, yes, we kept one!) We got called on a regular basis asking if we could take in a child, or children, because of some unfortunate circumstance. The stories of children in need were diverse as the children themselves. And of course those stories were never good stories.

Corey was one of the great kids we got to care for.

Linda, Kaley, and I discussed at great length, if we took in a child, however temporary it may be, would we be able to let go and give that precious child/children back. Our family had already been through so much emotionally, did we want to subject ourselves to more heart-tugging and heartbreaking.

On May 3, 2012, Linda called me while I was on the road for work stating they had a child - a two year old little girl - needing a home immediately with possible long term adoptive needs! Without really thinking I said, "Yes! Take her!". I later found out her name was Journey – the greatest name ever for a foster child.

It was already a crazy evening for Linda but it got crazier when Journey decided to jump off our stairs and smacked her eye. A deep cut opened just above her right eye and started bleeding! Linda called a neighbor to watch Kaley as she and Journey were off to the emergency room.

Remember this was just after Linda picked up Journey and brought her home! And as a foster parent you are always slightly nervous of doing anything that could be construed as irresponsible parenting; everything has to be reported - and this certainly was. I felt so bad for Linda who was once again taking all this on – alone - while I was gone working.

That's why we began calling Journey "fearless". She was always jumping off things and doing crazy stunts. To this day Journey still has a scar - and Linda also!

Kaley and Journey. Notice the scar on Journey's right eye.

Journey did not sleep through the night for the first six months: she screamed every night 3-5 times a night. She slept at the end of our bed so one of us – mainly Linda – could get up and hold her and rock her. It was tough. Linda didn't think she'd survive the lack of sleep every single night.

Journey was sometimes more than we thought we could handle (and still can be). But we also could never have imagined all of our health trials. There were days when Linda and I questioned if we did the right thing – not only for our family and all its circumstances but for this troubled little girl – by taking her in. Originally, I was still on the road traveling so that burden fell mainly on Linda. I know there were days when she felt so alone. She would call me, in tears, while I was working, upset about something Kaley or Journey did or said. I did my best to "just listen", and then not say something stupid. I know she felt helpless - and so did I.

A child's first two years of life are *critical* development stages. It became very clear that Journey's development had suffered greatly prior to being placed into our care when she was 2 ½ years old. She was not used to being taught right from wrong. Her "discipline" was abuse. And though she mastered shouting "No!" her vocabulary was limited.

We've told ourselves repeatedly, "It's not her fault. It's not her fault. It's not HER fault." We renewed our determination not to give up on her. Her world already had! After many - often heated - conversations Linda and I recommitted to loving this little girl with everything we had, even if it meant just telling her we love her over and over, and hugging her and not letting go.

*It is a brave act of valor to despise
death; but where life is more
terrible than death, it is the the truest valor to dare to live.*

~ Sir Thomas Browne ~

Ok... It Can Get Worse

Because of my ongoing health issues the state of Washington's Department of Social and Health Services (DSHS) would not renew our foster parent license; we wanted to help more kids but couldn't, and that was and still is depressing.

Despite the challenges I ended 2012 qualifying for Advisory Council (the top 6 producers!) which included an all-expenses paid trip for Linda and I to a beautiful resort in Scottsdale, AZ, the Fairmont Scottsdale Princess, in March of 2013.

For 2013 I also made Advisory Council and missed being #1 for the year on the last day of the year! The trip that year took us to North Miami, FL, and the Beacharbour Ocean Resort in March of 2014.

Bill, Rob, and Greg at the Awards Night dinner.

During the Spring of 2013 I was not really feeling well but I stubbornly kept working. Linda finally dragged me to my general M.D., who immediately checked me into the hospital. I would stay there for five days - with a fever of 104!*

It was very difficult physically, but more so mentally. I was quarantined. Though exhausted I could not sleep. If I did doze off I had the most disturbingly, realistic dreams. I literally was eating people and could taste, and feel, the person's *flesh* in my mouth. I became afraid to sleep! Apparently that's what narcotics do to me. That also meant I had few pain management options. The doctors couldn't figure out why I was going through all of this, and never did; oh, the story for much of my health history.

To this point Linda had been the stabilizer in the lives of the Herman family. But she began to feel "off balance" during the summer of 2013, something wasn't right. She went to her doctor. And that of course lead to another doctor - which you know by now is never good. She had hearing loss and her vestibular testing was abnormal. After an MRI she was diagnosed, not with with a brain cyst like Kaley, no she was diagnosed with a (benign) brain *tumor*! An acoustic neuroma. WHAT!???

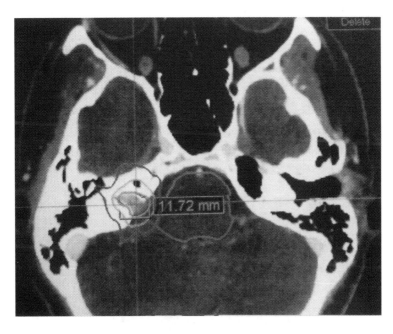

Once again, how was all of this possible!? Yet again we were in shock. Had our Guardian Angel left? The Good Lord was sure giving us just about as much as we could possibly handle without shattering.

As I mentioned earlier Linda has a medical background and takes great pride in researching everything she can about PKD, Kaley's brain cyst, her mom and dad's ongoing health issues, our friend's daughter's health challenge - to help anyone she can. So she dug right in researching all of her possible treatments, procedures, side effects, outcomes, and of course, the best doctors and hospital to have any treatments attempted anywhere in the U.S.A.

After all the research and numerous contacts – phone calls, emails – with various surgeons and specialists all over the country, Linda would opt for radiation treatments at Stanford University, in Northern California. She determined radiation was dangerous but brain surgery came with even greater risks.

Linda flew down first and took a few days to meet with everyone who would play a role in her procedure. The specialists at Stanford created a custom "helmet" for Linda. This helmet would precisely guide the radiated lasers to the tumor, all the while attempting to not damage any of the surrounding tissues. Kaley and I flew down two days later in time to take Linda to her treatments.

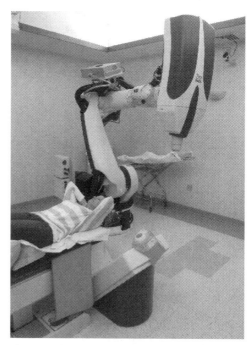

Linda, ready for radiation treatments. Her custom "helmet" is to her left.

Once again through the Grace of God, and some amazing doctors, the procedures were successful. Linda did lose some more hearing (she now wears a hearing aid) and still has some dizziness.

We have always tried to either shield the girls from the worst of our health stuff or turn a hospital visit out of state into a fun outing. This trip to San Francisco we made sure Kaley got to walk on the Golden Gate Bridge, tour Fisherman's Wharf, and see and learn about Alcatraz.

Since Journey was a Foster child, still officially in the state of Washington's custody, we were unable to get permission for her to leave the state to travel with us. We were able to find another foster family to watch her while we were in California.

2014 and I continued to work, which meant missing my family. It always hurt my heart pulling out of the driveway as the girls cried. I always hated when my dad had to leave on some business trip. During one trip to Bellevue, WA, I had just finished another long day of work and I was back at my hotel when I started not feeling well. I never worked a typical 8am – 5pm day. Since I handled my own schedule I often had days that began at a 7:00 am breakfast, with a dinner ending at 10:00pm, and plenty of meetings in between. I began feeling dizzy and light-headed. It got worse as everything began spinning around me. Then I began throwing up. It wasn't getting better as things were really spinning out of control. I needed to get to the E.R. but there was no way I was going to chance driving myself. So I called a cab, grabbed a trash can, and headed to the Emergency Room. Of course I threw up in the cab - in the trash can. I apologize to the driver, gave him a good tip, and went into the hospital.

After a night in the E.R. I was diagnosed with vertigo and tinnitus. (I thought I had tinnitus because my ears have been ringing so loud since I can remember.) I was released in the early morning with a cab ride back to my hotel. And yep, I - carefully - went back to working later that day. Never let anyone outwork you!

Later that same year I was also diagnosed with painful shingles. It was just one more thing to add to our long Herman family list of health challenges.

Since being able to foster care for Journey we had been working with the state trying to officially adopt her. After a lot of court maneuvering we finally got to adopt our beautiful Journey, who was now 4 years old - on 07-18-2014!! Linda, Kaley, and I went into court before a judge and swore to provide for this child all the love and support we possibly could for the rest of our lives. It was very emotional for everyone in the court. We all cried when the judge announced that the state of Washington, from that day forward, recognized Linda and I as the official parents, and Kaley as the official sister of Journey Alexa Herman!

It's official!

Journey kept asking us what was wrong and why were we all crying. We cried even more when we told her that we were now her mommy and daddy - forever. We promised her we would *never* let anyone, or anything, ever harm her again.

Again, please go to www.adoptuskids.org for more information on becoming a foster parent.

To celebrate we took a two week vacation to Florida. The first week was spent at Disney World. We stayed at a beautiful Marriott resort in Orlando. We then went on a Disney Cruise – the Disney Dream - to their private island. It was a great trip especially seeing Kaley's and Journey's faces light up with all the new and different experiences.

I again made Advisory Council, this time for 2014. That rewards trip was to Dana Point, CA, and the spectacular Monarch Beach Resort in March of 2015. This was an especially great trip because this time we took our two girls, and visited my sisters.

*Often it's the deepest pain which empowers
you to grow into your highest self.*

~ Karen Salmansohn ~

Thank God For A Table

As I mentioned, during my career a typical week meant leaving/ driving on a Sunday night to Seattle, WA, or Eugene, OR, etc., and then coming home on Thursday or Friday night. But on more than one occasion I left the house on a Sunday night – after putting the kids to bed at 8:30 pm, driving all the way to Seattle (3 ½ hrs!), realized I had forgotten my medications, and had to drive all the way back home. Then, yep, drive all the way back to my hotel! And then go the work the next morning for an 8:00 am meeting! Not fun.

Working had always kept my mind (mostly) off my health; I used it as a focus. I was still experiencing continuing migraines but now I had swelling in my legs, particularly during the second half of 2014 and into the new year. And yes, once again, no one knew why. One of the theories my many doctors were discussing was maybe, somehow, my native kidneys were causing at least some, if not all, of the swelling.

On April 15, 2015, Linda and I where coming back from an afternoon appointment with one of my surgeons where we discussed removing my native kidneys. (They usually do NOT take out the native kidneys – even huge PKD kidneys - when someone has a kidney transplant.) I was driving on Interstate 5 in Oregon when we decided to stop at a furniture store. Linda had been looking at a new kitchen table. As soon as I pulled into a parking space and turned off the car a sharp pain fired through my abdomen. I didn't know what was happening. Linda asked, "What's wrong?", and I told her I didn't know. The pain lasted 30 seconds or so before it subsided some. I sat for a minute and then decided to try to get out of the car and into fresh air. I felt a little better so we went into the store.

After a few minutes discussing the table with a salesperson my stomach was still not right so I left and walked gingerly to the bathroom. I suddenly had the feeling of diarrhea and then the incredibly sharp pains came roaring back – but if possible, much worse. Something was very wrong with me. As I stumbled out of the stall I almost passed out from the horrible pain. I remember thinking, "I'm going to die, right here, in this dirty bathroom."*

I struggled - ever so slowly - back to where I left Linda, but she was now at the counter apparenting buying the table. The salesman came over and offered me some water. I asked him to get my wife and the three of us debated calling an ambulance or what to do. Feeling only slightly better but *very* embarrassed by my commotion, I went to the car while Linda finished paying for the table. In the car the debate of going home or to the E.R. continued. I just wanted to go home and rest. (Yes, I can be a stubborn man.)

Thankfully, Linda wisely said, "We are going to the hospital!"

Linda dropped me off outside the Emergency Room at Legacy/ Good Samaritan hospital in Portland and she went to park. I shuffled through the doors and up to the attendant at the counter. She asked me, "What's wrong?" I told her, "I have severe, sharp, stomach pains."

What happened after that was a bit of a blur. I do remember the doctor talking to me about the need for emergency surgery but I don't remember him saying what for, or what he was going to do. Linda would tell me weeks later what the doctor said in detail. She always thought I knew everything, including all the details he described because I seemed alert and talking.

Diverticulitis = my colon had ruptured.

What if we would have not gotten off the freeway to go to the store? What would have happened if I was driving 65 mph on the interstate!? My Guardian Angel again. Unbeknownst to me at the time from that day forward my traveling for work was over. I would end up working from home, again, for at least the next 2 years.

Emergency surgery was performed by Dr. Jan that night at approximately 10:30pm. I woke up the next day with a 2 inch diameter hole left of my belly button and part of my bright red colon sticking out, called a stoma. I now had a colostomy. I would be pooping in a bag for possibly the rest of my life.

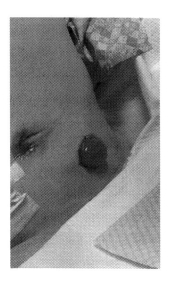

And my swelling only got worse while lying in my hospital bed. My legs and feet swelled up even more but it was now also greatly affecting my private area.

The nurse came in the next day to give Linda and I lessons on how to properly attach a ring to my body/skin and then a stool bag to the ring. She first asked me if I had "named it yet?" I didn't answer her as I was still not in the mood for jokes.

After a week or two my skin developed granulomas, which are painful growths usually due to infection. To remove a granuloma my wound specialist used cryotherapy – liquid nitrogen – to freeze the growths. Yes it stings but the granulomas always had to be eliminated.

Oh, but my health issues still weren't done because only about a month after my colon rupture surgery I began having severe pains over my transplanted kidney area – my lower right side. So Linda and I finally went – again - to the E.R. The doctor there told me I had some fluid build up in my abdomen. What!? I really didn't know what that meant. I was informed by both the doctor and my nurse that I would be checked into the hospital. Then, AFTER Linda went home to care for our girls the doctor told me I was being discharged! She only recommended I follow up with my general m.d. or nephrologist. I was not happy, particularly when I ended up having to take a cab home. Thanks for nothing as you'll learn.

As you can imagine I was still experiencing the pains for a few days as we attempted to get in to see a specialist. We were able to get an appointment with one of my surgeons who after seeing me – unexpectedly and immediately - checked me into the hospital. He thought I had a lymphocele which is where lymph fluid leaks out. So *that night* I had surgery to cut an opening, called a "peritoneal window", which allows the fluid to flow into the abdomen to be absorbed. This is a problem that can occur following a new transplant but not usually several years after. Yea me again!

But the fluid *didn't* absorb... and wouldn't.

While I was in the hospital recovering I was also having stomach issues so a doctor decided it was necessary to insert a tube into and through my nose and down into my stomach, called Nasogastric Intubation. (Once again... What!?)

My nurse instructed me to drink water using a straw, taking big gulps, and to not stop until the tube was all the way in. She then pushed the tube up into and through my nose, down my throat, and into my stomach. It was incredibly painful; I literally saw stars and such just like on cartoons when someone gets hit really hard.

It was no fun either when my doctor finally pulled the drainage tube out of me. At this point in my health history and being in that hospital bed, I had never felt so beat up. The recent kidney transplant and complications, my rupture/ostomy, this surgery to stop the fluid build-up, on-going swelling, then the drainage tube, and migraines were definitely taking their toll on me - physically and mentally. Dr. Bennett came to visit me the day they pulled the tube and said, "They've beaten you up pretty good haven't they?" I just looked up at him and answered, "Yep."

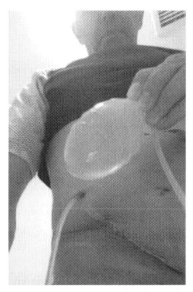

The constantly draining fluid. And the
scar from my kidney transplant.

Dr. William M. Bennett, MD, MACP, became very involved with
my medical journey when my transplant became complicated.
He always seemed to know when I was in the hospital fighting
this or that; and he seemed to always make a point to come see
me. Please allow me to tell you a little about this distinguished
human being.

As I mentioned earlier Dr. Bennett is the Medical Director, and
Transplantation Director for Renal Research, at Legacy Health
Systems, Portland, OR. With more than 40 years of experience,
Dr. Bennett is an expert in kidney transplantation.

Dr. Bennett received his medical degree from Northwestern University, Chicago. He retired as a Professor at Oregon Health & Sciences University in 1999. Dr Bennett is the current Editor-in-Chief Emeritus of the *Clinical Journal of the American Society of Nephrology.*

Dr. Bennett has more than 500 peer-reviewed publications to his credit and has contributed to 180 books and chapters. Dr. Bennett is a Master of the American College of Physicians, a Fellow of the American Society of Nephrology and has been its past president. He is also a fellow of the American Society of Transplantation.

Dr. Bennett has been honored for his contributions to the medical profession, including the Polycystic Kidney Research Foundation Jared J. Grantham Distinguished Achievement Award, the Belding Scribner Award of the American Society of Nephrology, the Kidney Association of Oregon First Gift of Life Award, the Medical Research Foundation of Oregon Discovery Award and Prize, the American Association of Kidney Patients

Medal of Excellence Award for his commitment to patient care, the Donald W. Seldin Award of the NKF for excellence in clinical nephrology and the Alumnus of the Year for Northwestern University Medical School. He has been identified as a nationally ranked top physician by *Portland's Top Doctors, America's Top Doctors,* and *Best Doctors in America.*

So you can see why I am so honored to have this incredible person on my side battling all my challenges. His expertise, particularly with PKD, has invaluable, and his connections at the Mayo Clinics provided us needed access and help.

After a few more days I was out of the hospital and back working from my home office. I somehow managed to increase sales for 2015 but for the first year since joining the company, I did NOT qualify for Advisory Council. I was extremely disappointed.

While all that was happening to me doctors discovered my dad's *second* cancer. This time it was prostate cancer. They found it early enough and with chemotherapy treatments – no surgery – they were able to eliminate it all. Praise Jesus.

I also had my first colonoscopy at age 50, as recommended. Dr. Barry DeGregorio, my gastroenterologist, put me out and went in through *my ostomy*. When I awoke my doctor told me everything looked good – no polyps, no bowel cancer. Then all of the sudden, stool started shooting out of my ostomy! I did not have a bag on yet. What a mess!! All the nurses were shocked. I was embarrassed. And Linda instinctually jumped into action and helped clean it, and me, up.

A few things worth noting about having an ostomy: I never could feel when it was time to go #2, or stop it; 'stuff' just came out into a bag attached to and hanging from my side whenever it wanted to. And when it filled I would go to the bathroom and empty the bag, which had an opening at the bottom. And yes if you must know there were times when the bag would fill completely when I wasn't close to a bathroom. I always feared the bag would explode! Thank God it never did.

Something else I could not control was the gas. Sometimes the bag would just fill up with gas like a balloon. I would need to go to a bathroom and let it out. Every time we went to church I would have to hold my hand tight over my ostomy attempting to hold in the gas, or at least keep it quite. More than once while in public it made "noises", and I would pray no one noticed.

But one specific time, of course when the pastor was praying so it was very quiet, it made a long loud noise. The younger man in front of us started cracking up. His wife or girlfriend nudged him to stop laughing. I was VERY embarrassed, but I can laugh at it now.

Whether due to the continuous fluid build-up in my abdomen, continuing structural weakening from PKD, or both I developed very large hernias around my ostomy and in my lower right groin - again. I had huge bulges across my lower stomach area. My pants did not fit. I would be wearing nothing but sweats for the next two years, even to church. (See "Area 51" in the back for pictures.)

When my fluid, or ascites, builds up it puts a very uncomfortable pressure on my stomach and lungs making it difficult to eat and breathe. I first got "drained", or paracentesis, when I was in the hospital recovering from a previous surgery. My G.I. doctor, Dr. Degregorio, then became much more involved with my case and these perplexing issues. Paracentesis is a hospital out-patient procedure where they take an ultrasound of the abdomen to see where the fluid is located and approximately how much. Individuals with liver cirrhosis often have this fluid issue, called ascites. The doctor marks with a pen where he or she wants to place the drain tube. Then comes the long lidocaine shot (painful!) into my side and through my abdomen wall to numb the area in order to insert the drain tube into my side.

The fluid - which looks like urine – is then pulled out. If they drain over 3 liters at any one time they put in an I.V. and give me albumin (protein). Quite often the drain tube gets caught on my intestine/bowel from the suction; it is *extremely* uncomfortable.

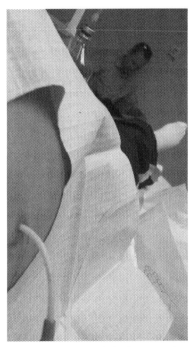

Rob's bloated stomach being drained.
Greg is in the background.

Per Mayoclinic.org, the peritoneal cavity is the largest fluid-filled cavity in the body and secretes approximately 50 milliliters of fluid per day. This fluid acts as a lubricant and has anti-inflammatory properties. On average I was being drained every 2 or 3 weeks, and 5 liters at a time. Understand that's equivalent to two and one half, 2 liter bottles of soda! Or 5,000 milliliters - when the human body produces just 50 ml a day!!

After the "peritoneal window" surgery, I began filling with fluid, having to be drained every 2 weeks and the amount kept increasing. Linda and I started going to specialist after specialist to determine what to do. At the same time I was losing weight, a lot of weight, which was also NOT good.

We reached out to the PKD Foundation who advised us (along with many others) to go to the Mayo hospital. However I was in no shape to be flying. Phoenix is a shorter non-stop flight then Rochester, MN so we ended up going to the Mayo Clinic in Scottsdale, AZ. It was somewhat frustrating as they didn't know us, and we didn't know their "system". We had to move all the records and tests to Mayo and then try to convince their specialists that the doctors in Portland had already ruled out liver issues, cancers, and other possibilities. In spite of all my previous tests - including a liver biopsy, an MRI, and CTs - they wanted their own test results.

All the scheduling, waiting, and appointments took months. We first went to Mayo the end of October for testing. It was then early December before kidney specialist Dr. Ray Heilman was able to see me. He too concluded taking out my native kidneys was the only hope I had for figuring out where my fluid was coming from. But he also felt the surgery would be very risky due to my compromised health and abdomen fluid. Dr. Heilman warned us fluid and surgeries don't mix well. He felt I might not survive.

With that information we flew back home but not before I had paracentesis which drained 10 liters. That is most I ever had drained at one time to date - 10 LITERS! And that time they did *not* give me albumin so while I was walking in the hospital lobby with Linda, I suddenly started to collapse and almost passed out. Linda reminds me often of how dire my situation was at the time. I didn't want to hear any of that so I purposefully ignored that type of bad news. I was just trying to survive by focusing on one day at a time.

The Mayo Clinic in Scottsdale, AZ.

*Life affords no higher pleasure than that of
surmounting difficulties, passing from one step of
success to another, forming new wishes and seeing
them gratified. He that labors in any great or laudable
undertaking has his fatigues first supported by hope
and afterward rewarded by joy.*

~ Samuel Johnson ~

2016 Things

Just a week or so after we flew home from Arizona is when my bowel started getting trapped in my hernia. That quickened conversations with Dr. Paul Andrews at Mayo who said he would have to put together a team to do the double nephrectomy surgery. But the tricky surgery couldn't be scheduled until Jan 19! Linda and I didn't know if I'd make it that long. Linda asked Dr. Andrews what we should do? He very matter-a-factly said, "If he can't get on a plane, I can't help you." Mayo was the only place to agree to try taking out my kidneys under these exacting circumstances.

The hernia, which is a tear or opening in the muscle, on my right side was extremely painful. I was often curled up on the floor. At the time I didn't know what was happening. I thought I may have food poisoning which I experienced in the past. My stomach hurt. I couldn't eat or drink. I started throwing up.

So once again Linda took me to the E.R. in Portland. It was December 30/31, 2015. I had my typical and now very familiar routine of getting a bed/room, vitals taken, and then nurses attempting to insert an I.V. for the pain. It usually took a second nurse to find a vein, and this time was no different.

After an ultrasound the E.R. doctor came in and explained my colon was pinched in the hernia, and it was preventing food to pass through to be digested. I had an obstruction! She began pushing on my hernia bulge, while at the same time she was talking to the nurse about preparing me for surgery. The last thing I and my body needed at that point was another surgery. Then without warning I felt a "pop". I instantly started to feel better. My bowel had literally been pushed back in. No surgery. And I was home for New Year's.

Almost six years since my kidney transplant I still had my fistula in my left arm. The doctors called it my "insurance policy"; in case my kidney ever failed I could still do dialysis. Because of the fistula nurses were not allowed to draw blood or give I.V.s in that arm. So my right arm became the workhorse. Many of the veins have shrunk, collapsed, and/or hardened over time.

But 2016 would believe it or not be my most eventful health year to date. Apparently we just hadn't had enough already - or my Guardian Angel was long gone.

After my December 30/31, 2015 E.R. visit I would have my next obstruction and trip to the E.R. *just a week later* on January 6/7, 2016. The "routine" was the same: check in, I.V. for pain, ultrasound, push on obstruction bulge while discussing emergency surgery, then "pop", and go home. If there was no "pop", they were prepared for surgery because I wouldn't live with an obstructed/blocked bowel.

Then on January 8/9, I developed a major migrain, and then another obstruction! The pain was intolerable. An I.V. was needed immediately, so Linda called 911, again. And once again the paramedics and fire department were at our home. Paramedics took vitals, inserted an I.V., and wheeled me out on a stretcher into the ambulance. We were off to the E.R. This time on the way to my hospital in Portland the paramedic told me the E.R. at Good Samaritan/Legacy hospital was was on "divert", meaning they were full and not taking anymore ambulance patients so we detoured to Legacy Emanuel hospital.

By the way, on average it cost us over $1000.00 for the paramedics to come, put in an I.V., and transport me to a Portland hospital.

After so many trips to the E.R. we feared I would have to have emergency surgery to fix my hernia and if that happened I'd never make it to Mayo to have my kidneys removed on January 19th, as that was apparently the last hope to getting better.

January 14 I checked in to the outpatient unit at Good Samaritan hospital for an ultrasound and had 5 liters of fluid drained.

January 17 Linda and I traveled to the Mayo Clinic in Scottsdale, AZ. My Mayo doctors still felt my native kidneys were somehow causing my ascites and their team was willing to attempt the risky surgery. On January 18 we went to see Dr. Andrews. Linda and I will never forget this appointment. He was going over my MRA results which showed some "changes" so he called his colleague in neurosurgery for a consult. We heard him say, "But these results shouldn't delay surgery to remove Rob's kidney's." After that brief conversation, Dr. Andrews very matter-of-factly said to me, "I'm afraid this surgery will kill you", and then he suddenly left the room. Shocked and puzzled I said to Linda, "Shouldn't he have a little more self confidence?" It was the first time we'd laughed in weeks - though we knew things were very serious.

Tuesday, January 19, I was waiting in preop when the anesthesiologist came in and introduced himself. At some point he said, "Your heart sure is pounding". My heart had been pounding hard for years since my fistula surgery; I just thought that was my "new normal", not my near death.

I was in surgery for several hours. Linda finally received a call saying everything went well. Dr. Andrews met with Linda to discuss the surgery. He said they saw my transplanted kidney was "weeping" lots of fluid; they felt it was the source of my problem. The doctor also relayed to us that while they were doing surgery they had someone keep a close eye on my heart monitors and rhythm. The team was able to apply cautery and cover the kidney with a type of gel. In other words, they attempted to *scar it, and glue it*, to stop the leaking. Dr. Andrews was very optimistic.

Dr. Dan Johnson, the second surgeon, then came out to speak to Linda. He repaired my large hernia and then described *in detail* how he tried to fix the peristomal hernia but explained it might not hold closed (and it wouldn't). He also related how they saw the fluid coming directly out of the transplanted kidney and that he'd "never seen this before". He was *not* optimistic and felt whatever was causing this anomaly would continue to be a problem. He was very cautious, stating this "fix might just be a bandaide."

The next day the pastoral staff came to visit us. They informed us Dr. Andrews had put them on standby during the surgery. OK - I guess it was kind of serious after all.

I did arrange ahead of time to have my polycystic kidneys donated to the PKD Foundation for research purposes. Please consider this option if you, or someone you know, needs their kidney(s) removed. (Contact www.pkdcure.org)

On the following Tuesday Dr. Ray Heilman, my transplant nephrologist in charge of my case called Linda's cell phone and said, "Mr. Herman needs his heart checked. We think his fistula might be causing cardiac failure, which can be causing his ascites too." They immediately added an echocardiogram and a heart catheterization test, just one week post op. The fistula was putting too much pressure on my heart. I had *high output cardiac failure,* a rare side effect of having a fistula. Yea me again!

The good news was that it could be reversed by taking down the fistula, meaning reversing the connection of the artery that was diverting fast flowing blood directly into the vein going back to the heart. Linda was asking one of my doctors what to do if this or that happened when he stopped her and said, "Lady, you have bigger fish to fry!" Meaning Rob's in bad shape, don't worry about this little fistula problem.

The next thing I know I'm taken to a room, my neck was numbed with a shot of something (painful), and then a wire goes into my neck and down into my heart to measure outputs and pressure. The results showed my heart was working dangerously too hard.

The next day in the afternoon two male nurses came in stating they would be removing my drainage tube from my side. Yes, it was still in from the surgery a week earlier. They pulled the tube out. Do you think the fluid just happened to stop flowing? Of course not. So I was told to hold a towel over the site and keep good pressure on it. I could see a debate was going on between these guys and then they asked me if would I rather have one needle poke or a few?

What?

Before I knew what was happening they removed the towel and I watched as one of the nurses stuck what looked like a hook with a string on the end into my skin near the opening - which was still leaking fluid. A sharp burning pain torn through my side. He then did it again, resulting in the same intense burning pain. He pulled on the hook and string, tied it in a knot, and said, "All done."

After trying to relax from that *mini torture session* I realized they had put a stitch in me to close the tube opening - without any lidocaine or any painkillers! What Linda helped me realize after was the debate the nurses had was whether they should go try to find some lidocaine or just sew me up without it, which is what they did!

Many of the doctors also felt the high cardiac output "could" also be causing my continuous fluid build up so the decision was made to squeeze in... this one more surgery. The thinking was, reduce my fistula, thus hopefully reducing the stress on my heart, and possibly slowing the fluid buildup. So the *next* day I had fistula reduction surgery! Yes, this was only a few days after they had taken out my kidneys and all the other stuff!

The doctors were trying to get as much done as possible before we were scheduled to fly home; and it seemed like they did! We flew home the next morning. That three hour flight felt like ten hours. I was beat up - again.

February was also full of more stomach pain and migraines, and no sleep. So my neurologist ordered a 24 hour sleep study. For those of you who have never experienced a sleep study please allow me to share my experience. My room had a small twin bed, a bad pillow, and no T.V. After I changed into my sleep attire the nurses hooked me up to many different wires, attached to many different areas over my body. Then they turned off the lights and told me to go to sleep. Oh, and if I had to go to the bathroom I needed to let them know so they could unhook me. Flashbacks of dialysis.

And the best part, the nurses were watching everything – I mean every snore, grunt, scratching, flopping around - from cameras, including infrared cameras, positioned around the room. Obviously the perfect conditions for a good night's sleep, right?

So of course I laid there... and laid there... for hours... thinking about the cameras and nurses watching my every move. And then I had to go to the bathroom. As the nurses unhooked me they also reminded me that I needed at least three consecutive hours of sleep to "qualify" as an official study. Otherwise I would have to do this all over again. No pressure for sure now!

After a non-restful but still qualifying sleep study, I was diagnosed with sleep apnea. We purchased a CPAP machine. Yea!

On February 29 (leap year!) I was confirmed to have Clostridium Difficile = aka, C Diff; a painful, serious bacteria infection of the intestines. With everything going on health wise, including this, I had lost a lot of weight – now 140 lbs down from my normal 185 lbs. I was given antibiotics and told to get lots of rest.

March would continue with many more on-going doctor visits: nephrologist, M.D., transplant specialists, G.I, sleep specialist, cardiologist. I also had stomach issues, migraines, and just being sick. I would also have itching fits where my back would become very itchy - for still unknown reasons - lasting a few days at a time. There was never any signs of rash or skin irritations. ???

April 11, I had fistula *reversal* surgery in Portland. Again, the doctors at Mayo, and here in Portland, now felt by *removing* the fistula completely it *may* reduce my fluid build up. Goodbye to my 'insurance policy'.

April 21 my painful C Diff came back which is not uncommon. Linda once again went to work researching C Diff fecal transplants. My doctor was hesitant because the procedure is only approved for really persistent cases.

May 4 I had another 5 liters of peritoneal fluid drained.

May 6 I had a C Diff fecal transplant. I know I said the same thing, "What is a C Diff f*ecal transplant*? And how is it performed?" A C Diff fecal transplant is where a doctor transfers one person's poop into the person who has C Diff, with the hope this new bacteria will fight off the C Diff. Yes, you read that write right = a poop transfer!!

Our tornado was now F6, and out of control.

As you can imagine both Linda and I were not thrilled with this news. Think about everything we had been through to this point. I was exhausted with everything, so I know Linda had had enough also. And the ones who also didn't deserve being in the middle of all of this were our two beautiful, tough girls – Kaley and Journey. So Linda was given a *poop collecting device*. But here's the thing, the date the doctors scheduled to perform "the transfer" was the date Linda *had* to poop – BEFORE the appointment. Not to get anymore personal with you but Linda wasn't the most regular of poopers. She also suffers from irritable bowel syndrome (IBS). No pressure, right?

But being the great wife she is she was able to go! Yeah Linda! (No, I'm not going to say, "You go girl!") We carefully drove the specimen down to Portland trying not to get poop all over us. (Kidding!) I was prepped for the transplant and the next thing I know the doctor is transferring Linda's poop into me - through my ostomy. At that very moment I could not have blamed my Guardian Angel for abandoning me/us.

A few weeks went by and most of my extremely painful intestinal issues cleared up. The transplant was demeaned a success. I said a thank you prayer for Linda's poop. You have to laugh at all this... "stuff'.

Yea, we made it half-way through 2016.

On June 22 we all flew back down to Arizona for my surgery at the Mayo Clinic to repair my severe inguinal hernia on my right side over my transplanted kidney. I was in the hospital for four days as this hernia was repaired with a lot of mesh. And during this surgery the surgeons looked at my previously diagnosed "weeping" fluid kidney. They found that it was not (or no longer) leaking any fluid. Again, what!?

Also while I was at Mayo I had a lymphangiogram procedure. They injected an "oil" into the artery in my upper right leg/groin area (ouch!), waited, and then took x-rays of some of my lymph system.

August 25 I had another paracentesis to drain 3 more liters.

September 13 I had an (another) "anxiety attack". I haven't even talked about these indescribable experiences.

Then the first Sunday in September we were coming home from church when Linda suggested we stop and look at a new house for sale, because we didn't have enough going on in our lives! We all instantly loved it. The next thing I know movers are at our house, and we moved. It certainly wasn't the best time to move but when would it be. During all the on-going craziness of our lives we were determined to stay a strong family and lead as normal of lives as possible. Our faith stayed strong. We never asked, "Why me/us?" Linda and I knew there was always someone, another family, out there dealing with worse 'stuff' than us and we told the girls that constantly. And still do today.

October 1 I started having severe pain and swelling in my right foot. It became worse and worse so back to the doctor I go. The conclusion = gout. Now with all these annoying complications transplant patients must always be vigilant in making sure any medications they take over the counter, or prescribed by a doctor, do not interfere with their immune suppression medications. And as it turned out most of the possible prescriptions available for gout don't play nice with my current meds. So I was told to drink lots of water, elevate my foot, and give it time. If needed take *some* acetaminophen (Tylenol) for pain. Great.

At this point I (and probably you as well) was thinking, "Thank God 2016 is almost over; enough IS enough."

But then on October 11 I received a call from my sister, Janice. She informed me my oldest sister Laura, had apparently collapsed at work and she was being taken to the hospital. Janice was heading to the hospital and said she would call us back when she had more information about Laura's condition.

About a half hour later she called back crying and said simply, "She's dead." I yelled, "She died!?" The girls were also in the room, heard me yell, and immediately started crying uncontrollably.

I didn't know what to do. To say I was in shock would not do the conditions justice. Laura was the oldest. She had always been the rock that kept our family together when Mom had her massive stroke. We knew Laura had PKD but her kidneys were still functioning. My sister died at the young age of 56 from a cerebral (brain) hemorrhage caused by Polycystic Kidney Disease, just like Mom.

PKD had stolen yet another one of our family members.

I do not know if Laura was ever prescreened for aneurysms but with today's technology there is no excuse not to be. PLEASE get screened for aneurysms. A CT scan or MRI is simple, painless, and is covered by most, if not all, insurances.

My dad and his wife Sylvia happened to be in town for my nephew's upcoming wedding. The three of them - Dad, Sylvia, and Laura - met for lunch at In-and-Out. Laura went back to work and a few minutes later died - probably before she hit the floor.

To this day I don't think it was a coincidence that my Dad and Sylvia were in town (they live in PA), the three went to lunch, to In-and-Out (our favorite burger place), before she died quickly never knowing what hit her. Her Guardian Angel at work?

We all have to go someday; Please Lord, when it's my time that's the way I want to go; my last supper at In-and-Out and then - boom - it's painlessly over.

The four of us flew down to Southern California. I spoke at Laura's funeral. I told a story of how she was my mom growing up after Mom's stroke; how she used to force me to take showers when I was ten years old. Most ten year old boys don't want to take baths or showers! So I would run the water but never pull up the redirector so water would come out the shower head. I know, not smart! I would just sit on the toilet never getting in the water and wait a few minutes. Then I'd turn the water off, get dressed for bed, and walk out of the bathroom.

Standing there would be my second mom, my sister Laura. She would ask me if I actually showered and I would of course say, "Yes!" - with a huge attitude. Laura would check the shower walls for wetness and then ask, "How can everything be dry if you took a shower?"

Yes, I ended up showering.

RIP Sis.

In Loving Memory of

Laura Schumann
December 5, 1960 – October 11, 2016

"a woman who fears the Lord is to be praised" Proverbs 31

On October 25 I had a bone density test which confirmed osteoporosis. Doctors said it was most likely caused by all the medications I have been taking. My migraines which had become more frequent also continued to harass me.

November 6/7 I spent another night in the E.R. with another painful bowel obstruction, but on my left side.

Then on November 24, yep, Thanksgiving the paramedics were back to our home, this time the new house. I was back in the Emergency Room yet again. And yes again I was suffering from yet another bowel obstruction.

I was scheduled for another hernia surgery at the Mayo Clinic in AZ in early December. This time the operation would be on my left side around my ostomy. Linda and I grew concerned that I may not be able to fly because of the ongoing painful obstructions and possibly have to reschedule the surgery. Anyone who has ever dealt with scheduling with doctors knows you don't want to cancel any scheduled appointment, or it will take *months* to get back in.

So I decided to change my flight and fly out a day earlier by myself because I happened to be feeling good enough to travel; it was Wednesday, November 30. I landed in Phoenix, got my rental car, and exhausted, made it to my hotel. I said a quick 'thank you' prayer. But maybe my prayer was too quick because, believe it or not I once again started having those horrible obstruction pains. There I was laying in my hotel room, the pain getting worse and worse. And I was once again wondering to myself, "How *all of this* is possible?" But never asking "Why me/us, Lord?"

I ended up driving myself to the Mayo Clinic Emergency Room that night! The drive was only a few miles but it sure seemed much longer. When I checked in to the E.R. they asked me how I got to there. I told them I drove myself. They said almost in unison, "Not smart."

I was once again given an I.V., and then a CT. That took a few hours but once the E.R. surgeon saw my scan he and the nurses began discussing the need for surgery that night; the story of my life. It was around 10:00 pm. Remember it was Wednesday night. I informed him I was already scheduled for surgery sometime on Friday. (At the Mayo Clinic you have to call the night before your surgery to find out what time you are scheduled for.)

The E.R. surgeon was able to get in touch with my Friday surgeon. That surgeon said he could move some things around on his Thursday schedule in order to accommodate the need for my surgery a day earlier. The next day they repaired my large ostomy hernia. While I was there one of my many doctors recognized me and ask, "What brought you back *this* time?" I explained my current situation and then added, "I'm just trying to get all my health issues out of the way so that I'm healthy when I'm old." He laughed and said, "I like your thinking."

Linda flew out that Thursday and met me in recovery. I was released from the hospital on Sunday, December 4, 2016 and we flew home.

2016 finally came to a close. Yes, I was still working from home during this time. My sales numbers for 2016 were up again but not where the company wanted them. My position required 90% travel so working from home was not meeting that expectation. Signs were starting to show that my career may be over. Human Resources warned me the company "accommodating" me might be over.

2017 would be slightly less eventful though all the nagging things would continue. Now to this point in my life all the doctors/surgeons/specialists and tests still had not found the cause of my ascites. To that point they had all tried varying tests and surgeries but the general consensus still is there is no general consensus. Just because I received a kidney transplant AND then had my native kidneys removed did not mean I was free from Polycystic Kidney Disease. I have been told, and ultrasounds have shown, my liver has PKD cysts.

I have also been screened more than once and still show no signs of any brain aneurysms. Praise Jesus.

During the years following my colon rupture my blood work results were consistently in range of where my doctors wanted them. That meant my new kidney was doing its job. But my doctors, both here in Portland, as well as at the Mayo Clinic in Scottsdale were all still searching for an answer as to why this kidney may or may not be leaking and/or somehow causing the leaking. My Mayo doctors in Arizona also conferred with their colleagues in Minnesota regarding my continuing dilemma. As it has been put to Linda and I more than once, "Rob is one for the research books and case studies."

The discussions then turned to the possibility of another kidney transplant to try to stop the fluid buildup. The challenge with trying to get another deceased donor kidney was that my numbers were too good. The United Network for Organ Sharing (UNOS) does not give someone a way to get on the transplant list if their kidney output numbers are good but causing problems by leaking fluid or causing fluid build up.

So we began looking into the possibility of finding a living donor. We joined Kidneybuzz (www.Kidneybuzz.com), along with a lot of the kidney dedicated online discussion groups. A living donor is the most beneficial way to go for a transplant. There is obviously less wait time which also means less, or no, dialysis; the kidney is healthier; living donor kidneys last twice as long versus those from a deceased donor. The costs associated with a transplant are paid for by the recipients insurance. And donating does NOT increase other health risks, or shorten the donors life.

For more information being a living donor, please go to www. transplantliving.org, or organdonor.gov/about/process/living-donation.html.

Linda talked to our church pastor. He told us he would make an announcement to the congregation. The Sunday came, he prayed and explained our situation. To our surprise, though we should not have been, after the service a few people asked us about organ donation. One individual, Jeff Graham, who we did not know at the time stepped up to offer his kidney to me – a stranger.

Friend, and organ donor, Jeff Graham.

On April 16, 2017 I flew to the Mayo Clinic in Scottsdale for four days of more tests and to go through the evaluation process for a possible living kidney transplant. One of the doctors I met with looked me in the eyes and promised me they would find an answer for my ascites. He told me, "That's what the Mayo Clinic does, finds answers to the most challenging of cases... and yours certainly is."

For the first time in a long time I actually felt a little hope, a little burst of energy. I guess I had grown so accustomed to specialists, doctors, and surgeons telling me "we don't know", or that "the test didn't tell us anything new." He, and others, then referred my case to the top kidney specialists and surgeons at Mayo in Rochester, MN - which is their main hospital/campus. I was becoming more famous, or infamous.

But all the doctors who knew about my case, including here in Oregon, and Arizona, and in Minnesota did agree a new kidney might not be the answer and that removing a good, working kidney would not be wise. So for now that option has been shelved. And I am thrilled for my donor angel - Jeff. My goal and prayer are that he NEVER has to donate his kidney to me.

On May 25 I was asked to give my resignation at work, and did. For insurance we are temporarily on COBRA insurance (Consolidated Omnibus Budget Reconciliation Act of 1985 passed by Ronald Reagan). We are looking for permanent coverage.

Linda's dad, Lester Troyer, who was the rock of the Troyer family, had been fighting breast cancer also during this time. Yes, breast *cancer*, which added to everyone's pain and stress levels! The "tornado" just kept getting bigger. Lester/Dad was as strong as an ox. He built their home, had a farm, and most importantly helped the community every chance he could. He helped me/us every chance he could.

We were at his home on Sunday for a family dinner. Anyone who owns a farm or works on one knows there are *always* plenty of chores to do. Everyone was concerned that Dad was doing "too much" work on the property considering his health. He was now always exhausted which that was not his norm. I had a conversation with Linda's Aunt Ida saying, "If he (Dad) died today on his tractor he would die happy doing what he loved."

The next day Linda received a call from Aunt Ida saying there had been an accident involving Dad. He somehow rolled his tractor in a place he drove that tractor thousands of times before. The newer tractors are required to have a roll bar but his was an older tractor and it did not.

Dad was killed.

Linda cried like I had never heard her cry. I thought about what I had said the day prior, praying to Jesus Christ it was true: that he died doing what he loved. And that he is in Heaven.

You now know I am no fan of funerals and Dad's was no different. The Troyer family decided to have an open casket. I stayed out of the room and talked with the guests. I like remembering Dad as I do, and not lying in a box. (No disrespect to anyone else choosing an open casket.)

The funeral was on June 3. I was very proud and honored to be one of the pallbearers. I also wanted to speak at his funeral though it was difficult. It was important to me to remind everyone present that day just how giving Lester Troyer was and how strong of an individual he was. The Troyers come from a big Amish community so they filmed the event for those who could not travel to attend. RIP Dad.

Grandpa Lester Troyer.

Dad died the day *prior to* finding out he was to be honored with a Lifetime Achievement Award for the state of Oregon from the Lions Clubs International. An award few individuals have *ever* been graced with. During the funeral he was given his award posthumously. I was not surprised at all he chosen for such a distinguished award. Well deserved good shepherd.

On June 8, 2017 Linda and I went to Oregon Health & Science University (OHSU) in Portland for a lymphoscintigraphy procedure. A what!? I can't say it either! Yes this was yet another test to try to find where my fluid was coming from.

There was a bright picture window artwork on the ceiling above me as I laid on the procedure table/bed. Though it was a photo it looked liked an actual aquarium with lots of beautifully colored fish. The specialist informed Linda and I what was about to happen; it didn't sound like fun when he told me, "And it is going to hurt."

The specialist then asked if I, "was ready?" What was I going to say!??? So I bravely replied, "Yep". Then the male nurse told me to try not to kick him. What? He then proceeded to hold down my feet with a good amount of force. The specialist then injected a blue dye into the webbing between my big toe and second toe on my left foot. While he was injecting me he kept saying, "I know it hurts, it hurts, it hurts, it hurts." It took a long five seconds or so. It stung like I can't describe as I fought to keep my eyes from watering = ok, crying! Then the same "sting" between the second and third toes on the left foot. And the same words from him and my same reaction. Now I know why they have a male nurse hold down your feet and legs.

I was given a moment to catch my breath at which time I concentrated on counting all the fish in the picture window above my head. I said to Linda, "56". She responded, "What?" I told her, "There are "56 fish in the picture." She smiled, confused. I told her, "I need something to focus on. This really hurts", still trying to stay tough.

Next followed two more injections into my right foot.

I couldn't believe we were finished, at least with the pain part. Next was a special scan which would hopefully show any indications of a leak in my lymph system. The blue dye was barium - sulphate used to enhance images of my lymphatic system. The lymphatic system is an important part of one's overall immune system, and health, since the (lymph) fluid takes waste from tissue back to the heart. Anyone taking immune suppression medications knows our immune systems are already compromised to avoid the body attacking the foreign material – the transplanted organ(s).

But the procedure, like all the others before this one, showed no signs of any leaks. That was good news but also bad news. Once again it was another test that did not find the source of what is causing my fluid build up. I was back to feeling a little depressed, a little more beaten down.

Have I not commanded thee? Be strong and of good courage; be not afraid, neither be thou dismayed: for the Lord thy God is with thee whithersoever thou goest.

~ Joshua 1:9 ~

Ah, You Left Open My Incisions

Linda and I then flew to the Mayo Clinic, this time in Rochester, MN, on Sunday, July 16, 2017. A friend watched Kaley and Journey at home. On Monday morning during our very first appointment we met with the head surgeon and expert on kidneys at Mayo. He told us he had examined my complicated health history, admitting my case was well known to many. He unfortunately also admitted he had no answers to my ascites issue and that I "may just have to live with it". Always trying to find some positive perspective I took (and still take) some weird comfort in knowing that, at the very least, I have baffled some of the best minds in Oregon, Arizona, and Minnesota. Only 47 more states to go!

The Mayo Clinic in Rochester, MN.

After a few days of tests and meetings with more doctors I went in for surgery the morning of Thursday, July 20 to reverse my ostomy. At the same time they were going to attempt to repair its surrounding huge hernia, all while somehow managing a great deal of infectious fluid.

The head surgeon told Linda the surgery was a success. They reversed my ostomy. I would once again be going #2 the normal way again! They also repaired my extensive hernia using a lot of mesh. (For pictures, see "Area 51" in the back of the book.)

They also drained 5 more liters of fluid during the surgery. The ascites has been tested multiple times over the past years for cancers and other invasive matter. So far everything seems to indicate the fluid is just what it is supposed to be. Everyone has this peritoneal fluid in their abdomen. I am unexplainably producing too much of it. The other concern has always been that *any amount of* fluid around an incision is simply a huge risk of infection.

I woke to see my stomach area packed with black sponges and a drain tube coming from the the area. I was expecting to see my stomach covered with white gauze and bandages just like after all of my other surgeries. Since I was not sure why I had black sponges covering my incisions I asked my nurse. She informed me the surgeon left the incisions open. He did not suture his surgical openings closed. Asking if that was "normal?", she replied some surgeons choose to leave ostomy wounds open so they can "heal from the inside out." Interesting. Yea me again. (See "Area 51" in back for picture.)

I also had 2 other drain tubes sticking out of my right side connected to suction containers to collect the ascites/fluid. Like all my major surgeries the containers constantly had to be emptied by the nurses. Almost as fast as they could empty the collecting containers, the containers would fill right back up again. They were pumping I.V. fluid into me as fast as the fluid was draining out.

After a few days they pulled the catheter and one of my drainage tubes. I then had to learn to go to the bathroom all over. Though I needed to go I could not control going #1 or #2. I had no control over my rectum and urethral muscles. It was difficult and very frustrating. I would sit on the toilet and pray -beg to go to be able to go to the bathroom.

I was in the hospital for 6 days.

A nurse removed my remaining drainage tube in my right side as well as the sponges and drain in my incisions. That was the first time I truly understood that my surgical incisions were left wide open. This was a huge psychological shock to look down and see my stomach incisions open and ½ -1 inch deep. These open incisions had to be repacked daily. In fact Linda and I were taught how to pack, unpack, and then repack the wounds which initially was a pretty overwhelming task for me. But Linda, always my hero, would once again do what had to be done.

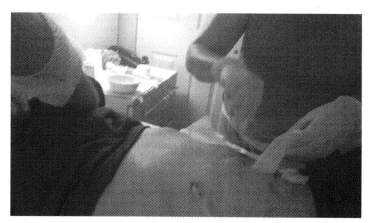

My recovery in the hotel. Linda packing
my wounds. Drain tube still in.

As I recovered Linda flew back to Washington to get the girls. We wanted Kaley and Journey to experience the fun and beauty of Minnesota. They all flew back to check me out of the hospital and into a hotel. It was nice to have the entire family with me as we spent another 5 days in the hotel while I recovered enough to fly back home. I still had a drain in my side that needed to be emptied constantly. My wounds also had to be packed/repacked in the hotel.

It took about 3 months for my incisions – a hole from the ostomy on my left and a seven inch incision going awkwardly down from my belly button - to close back together. My wound specialist, Deborah, did a great job helping me heal but I'm still left with some (more) nasty scars.

One other aspect of ostomy reversal surgery is the time it takes to reteach and rebuild the muscles that control bowel movements. The length of time it takes ones "pipes" to function again has been surprisingly frustrating to me but not to my specialists. This recovery has taken many months, and more of my patience. As my mom would often say, "Patience is a virtue"; now I know why.

In November 2017 Kaley (12) started having blood in her urine that lasted for about a week. Now what!? After a doctor visit and an ultrasound she was diagnosed officially with Polycystic Kidney Disease. We suspected it when she had her brain cyst surgery. But now my/our greatest fear had been confirmed: I had passed on this insidious disease (ADPKD) to our only biological child.

As you know there are two kinds of PKD: ADPKD – the "adult" version, and ARPKD – the "baby" version. So why is KK feeling the effects of ADPKD at twelve years old?

We are trying to find that answer. We had KK genetically tested. They did gene (DNA) sequencing on her. What they uncovered has put her in the medical books (Yea? Just like me). Kaley Shea

Herman is the first person *ever* to be discovered with an extra "T" cell in her PKD sequencing. What does that mean? They don't know. Why does she have this difference? They don't know. What's the next step? We just don't know...

On December 14, 2017 I had another ultrasound and then another 4.6 liters of fluid drained from my abdomen.

Happy New Year 2018!

Kaley and Journey went ice skating on January 2 and Journey broke her right tibia – her larger shin bone,; a *spiral* fracture. She slipped and fell on the ice and her leg got caught underneath and behind her. When I met up with them at the E.R. she was in good spirits. She told me she heard a "pop" and thought it was broken. This was before her x-rays.

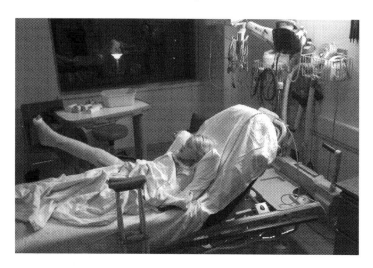

Also during January, 2018 my migraines resurfaced but now I was also waking up with them in the middle of the night. My blood pressure unexpectedly went up: 151/101 average and low pulse: 53. I wonder why!? (Sarcasm.)

On January 23 I couldn't take the migraine pain any longer so once again Linda took me to the E.R.

My migraines were now lasting for a week at a time!

My next surgery that I know of, should be to repair yet another hernia – this one is four inches or so above my belly button. My doctors here don't want to touch it right now due to all of my issues, particularly the ascites. Plus I need a long break from hospitals. So until this surgical repair I will continue wearing my abdominal binder so the hernia does not get any larger.

Kaley and Journey recently made the glorious decision to accept Jesus Christ as her Lord and Savior! They will be baptized soon. And I plan to be baptized again right along with them.

March 28, 2018 and I had severe pain and swelling in my left foot. I couldn't sleep. My gout had returned in the other foot. In most people gout tends to affect just the big toe. My gout affects all the toes, the entire foot, and up the ankle. Yea me, again! This time doctors loaded me up on the steroid, Prednisone.

My second birthday, or my kidneyversary (9 years!) was on April 4!

Friday, April 13 brought 31 Botox injections into both shoulders, the back of my neck, back of my head, temples, and then the brow of my forehead. My pain management doctors are trying a little preventive medicine to halt these destructive migraines.

America's future will be determined by the home and the school. The child becomes largely what it is taught, hence we must watch what we teach it, how we live before it.

~ Jane Addams ~

The Emotional Toll

Sharing my family's multi-generational life story has been therapeutic. Maybe I do need therapy!? I never realized the totality of my life's "adventure" beginning on that riotous Friday, the 13th. The self-evaluation has also been enlightening. But if I am going to share with you many of the Herman physical ailments I need to be honest and expose the *behind-the-scenes* emotional side as well. Because as any family dealing with chronic illness - physical or mental - knows it's the "stuff" that's hidden in the closet that no one ever wants to expose to light, let alone the public! We all know it's extremely difficult to be the person going through the physical problem(s). But one could also argue the loved ones having to watch that person dealing with their struggle(s) is just as difficult. So there is plenty of "suffering" to go around. And that suffering brings frustration, even anger, which can surface in an array of ways.

When I met Linda on that plane trip home, and then enjoyed our first (cold) date at the fair I knew I would need to tell her about PKD. Maybe she does but I don't remember when I finally told her about Polycystic Kidney Disease. I also told her of my family's long history fighting – and losing to – it, and my battles at the time that were unbeknownst to us really just beginning. I do remember her handling the news as an individual determined to help me face whatever our future together would bring 'in sickness and in health'. But we knew it was not going to be easy.

The thing about PKD, and any serious illness, is that when imperfect human beings are faced with extraordinary circumstances lasting day after day, month after month, year after year, it takes a toll emotionally. My mom and dad had their (un)fair share of yelling matches. It seemed they tried to argue at night when they thought I was asleep. I HATED hearing them. It ripped me up. But I also I wanted to join in the screaming. I wanted, I needed, to "vent".

And I never realized that - ever so slowly - PKD was stealing my energy reserves over the years; I was naive to the constant nagging of it all. I just worked harder. No excuses, right?: Never Give In! But I *was* making excuses for the way I was treating the people closest in my life. I was certainly failing Linda. I "vented" on her all too often whether it be regarding my health, my work, our home, and ALL those other wonderful *"little things"*.

And when Kaley became ill with her headaches, brain cyst, and PKD diagnoses, *that* became a source of tension. Then add in Linda's tumor, plus a fearless little girl named Journey - with all kinds of issues, and any little spark set off quite a spectacle of fireworks.

Ironic as it is Journey was the one who began shouting, "Stop fighting!" (But she yells that even if we're just talking!) Kaley tends to keep things inside.

We have our share of arguments like any relationship that has strong feelings and emotions does. We try to keep our heated conversations away from the girls ears but that's not always easy to do. Many arguments we seemed to have were over the dumbest things, which looking back, meant there was more to it than, say, who didn't fold the laundry or clean the dishes or whatever.

As you can imagine during the worst of our health stuff we did not have a truly happy home. We were so focused our physical healing we missed the fact we were unhealthy emotionally. We needed to open our eyes to what we were doing to each other and why. The true tension was the bills, the exhaustion, the aches and pains, the anger of constantly not feeling good, feelings of helplessness, being alone, etc.

And then someone said, "It's not fair!" Well, whether it's all "fair" or not, can't be changed by anyone - but Jesus.

Are things perfect today? No, and they never will be perfect. No one should have that expectation of any human being. But yes, it is perfect for us!

As I was finishing this chapter someone on a transplant survivors group happened to post the following question, *"Has anyone experienced relationship issues after a transplant or serious illness?*" There were hundreds of responses to this intriguing and revealing inquiry. Below are representative of the typical reply:

"Still together, had ups and downs."

"Separated from 22 yr friend and wife. It was many years of meanness I put her through."

"If I want to get rid of a guy I tell them I just had a lung transplant." (You can obviously look at this two different ways.)

A young person wrote: *"While I have never been in a relationship I have a hard time making friends. People in school stopped talking to me when I had a liver transplant."*

"Yes, I have been mean, but don't realize it."

"Not me, my wife saved my life!"

"Too much baggage that no one is gonna want to deal with me and my problems."

I was saddened by some of the replies and encouraged by others! But they all make the point we are trying to make: we understand what our fellow sufferers, and families, are constantly going through. None of us should have to feel alone. If nothing else reach out to me. My email is NakedintheMiddleofaTornado@ gmail.com. And no one should have to spend the energy trying to show a perfect public persona while their own "tornado" is hidden in a closet. *That...* is exhausting!

So please remember as I like to say, "We know what it's like to be naked in the middle of a tornado and all kinds of 'stuff' flying at us, with nothing to hold on to... but each other."

Regrets

People on their deathbed are often asked, "Do you have any regrets?" Well, since you know me so well now, I thought I would share two more things (before *my* death bed comes):

My #1 biggest regret: not having more children, like Kaley, and not being able to save more children like Journey.

*My #2 **biggest regret:** passing on our family's nasty Polycystic Kidney Disease (PKD) to Kaley, and making Linda have to deal with it all.*

Success is to be measured not so much by the position that one has reached in life, but as by the obstacles which he has overcome while trying to succeed.

Booker T. Washington

Timeline

1918: Demeter – double agent, escapes to Poland
1921: Herman's and Kula's, arrive in America
1928: Bako's arrive in America (PKD)
1938: Robert J. Herman, my dad, born
1939: Patricia Ann Bako, my mom, born
1959: John Bako Jr. dies - PKD
1965: Robert Patrick Herman born
1971: Broken collar bone
1974: Mom's stroke from PKD. Uncle's molestation
1977: Dad's foot cancer
1979: My scoliosis surgery. PKD?
1980: Slid down mountainside
1983: Graduate high school. Ran over a guy.
1984: Oral surgery. Hot grease on face. I move out.
1988: Mom's seizures
1989: Mom dies - PKD
1995: Rob's PKD "official"
1996: First hernia surgery, right side
1997: Meniscus surgery, left knee. MVP Award
1998: Second hernia, left side. "Employee of the Company" Award
1999: Met Linda.
2000: #1 in sales
2001: #2 in sales. Laid off.
2002: Married!
2005: Kaley Shea Herman born! Advisory Board

2006: Placed on Transplant list. Advisory Board

2007: Century Club = $100mm or more in sales!

2008: #1 = Century Club. Great Recession

2009: Fistula surgery. Dialysis. Kidney transplant! Advisory Board

2010: "Miscarriage". Kaley's brain surgery. Laid off.

2012: Foster parents/Journey. Advisory Council

2013: 104 degree fever. Linda's brain tumor. Advisory Council

2014: Vertigo. Shingles. Journey adopted! Advisory Council

2015: Diverticulitis/colostomy. Ascites. Obstruction. Advisory Council

2016: Obstructions. Ascites. Native kidneys out – Mayo - AZ. Fistula reduction surgery. C diff/transfer. Fistula reversed surgery. #3 Hernia surgery– Mayo. Osteoporosis. Sister Laura dies- PKD. Gout

2017: Retired. Dad – Lester Troyer dies. Lymphangiogram. Ostomy and hernia surgery– Mayo – MN. Ascites. Kaley- PKD.

2018: E.R. - Journey breaks leg. Migraines - 31 Botox injections. Gout numerous times. Ascites.

The Herman's Today:
Journey, Rob, Linda, Kaley

I wrote this book with the hope our story will inspire others with health issues to "Never Give In". We know Polycystic Kidney Disease (PKD) is horrible, not just because of cysts on our kidneys and liver and brain... but because of the entirety of the disease on the human body. Besides every disease, both physical and mental, is horrible and causes horrible side effects. I do realize that day to day struggles can eventually add up to what seems like a lifetime of combat; trust me I know this with you. My mom certainly had to feel that way. But that doesn't mean we can't try to enjoy something from each day and accumulate those days into the life you strive for. And if you can't pull something good from a lousy day then let it go by just knowing, if nothing else, that you beat it simply by surviving.

My life has been driven by faith, love, pride, stubbornness, naivete', and not knowing when to shut my mouth. But I also have lifetime career sales of over $1 billion! (Yes, that's a "B".) I want the second half of my life to be driven by more faith, more love, more humility, more ears, and by less stubbornness, less naivete', and less mouth. There is a reason why I am still here on this earth. (I pray He reveals it to me soon!) I truly believe I have, for some reason, been blessed well beyond what I ever deserved.

<u>Jeremiah 29:11</u> [11]"For I know the plans I have for you," declares the LORD, "plans to prosper you and not to harm you, plans to give you hope and a future." (NKJV)

One time when I was in the hospital my sisters were able to fly up to visit me. I remember sitting up in my bed, feeling like crud, my sisters sitting in chairs in front of me and we were discussing Linda and Kaley (we did not have Journey yet). I cried, they cried, as I explained how incredibly blessed I am to have Linda and Kaley for my family, as my life. I would certainly be a lost soul without them and Journey. Someone up above knew this when they put Linda and I together that day on the plane.

Almost 100 years ago The Herman's, and Bako's came to America – the land where dreams come true... and I believe wholeheartedly. From my grandfather - John, to my mother - Pat, to me - Rob, and now our daughter - Kaley, the Herman/Bako battle against Polycystic Kidney Disease (PKD) is not likely to end anytime soon. But when you, your loved ones, and your friends, join us standing shoulder to shoulder with us any battle becomes a fight we will win.

Family Photos:

Reminders

Please be an organ donor. You will <u>not</u> need your organs in Heaven. Go to: <u>www.organdonor.gov</u>, or <u>www.gorecycleyourself.com</u>.

Please consider being a foster parent. Go to: <u>www.adoptuskids.org</u>

And if you ever feel alone, and/or if you ever feel like hurting yourself... or someone/something else... PLEASE... call this National Suicide Prevention Lifeline Phone Number:

1 800 273-8255
<u>https://suicidepreventionlifeline.org</u>

Please consider accepting Jesus Christ into your heart.

A powerful agent is the right word. Whenever we come upon one of those intensely right words in a book or newspaper the resulting effect is physical as well as spiritual, and electrically prompt.

~ Mark Twain ~

Poems and Lyrics

Mirrors

I can't deny what's inside
The mirror portrays an imagine
It might not be
What I want to see
From myself, I cannot hide

Superman, I claim to be
Clark Kent stares back
So I shatter the mirror
With a burst of terror
Who controls the illusions I see

Mirror, Mirror
Who am I?
Mirror, Mirror
No time to cry
Mirror, Mirror
Who is he?
Mirror, Mirror
I don't want to be

One day it shows a look
The next, figures of distortion

Is it my mind that's crazy?
Or the mirror that's hazy?
I don't want a second look

Everyday I live this horror
With broken mirrors I can't escape
Maybe windows to some other place
That my mind will not erase
Reality or nightmare, I can't be sure

What You'll Never See In Me

I've got dreams
and not only when I'm sleeping
I got pride
so don't get in my way
I've got patience
and yes, it's a virtue
I've got confidence
if only I could let it go
I've got desires
Am I thinking of you?
But most of all...
I'm human...

And this is what you'll never see in me

I've got fun
and I want to share it with everyone
I've got style
it's not only in my hair
I've got hope
and not only for tomorrow
I've got to give
because giving is what I do best
I've got time
and it could only be for you
But most of all...
I love...

And this is what you'll never see in me

Why Must I Cry?

This world has so much beauty
But then on the other side
This world has so much destruction
And it only makes me cry

In certain countries peace is reality
It's something in which they take pride
Others live with fear and terror
And this is why I cry

(Pre-chorus)
A tear in a mother's eye
may mean pain and sorrow
While that same tear
may mean faith and hope for tomorrow

(Chorus)
I cry for the joy
I cry for the pain
I cry when we destroy
Sometimes I cry in vain

We say we're in love with each other
But at times we try to deny
This experience that's so mysterious
I am broken down and cry

All of us are unique and individual
Built both weak and strong inside
Don't let this beauty be turned away
Because you're never too old to try

(Pre-chorus)
A tear in a child's eye
may mean pain and sorrow
While that same tear
may mean faith and hope for tomorrow

(Chorus)

I cry for the joy
I cry for the pain
I cry when I destroy
Sometimes I cry in vain

Thank YOU for reading our story! Our goal is that it will move you to, at least, one new action in your life.

As Cicero once said,

> "Gratitude is not only the greatest of virtues,
> it is the parent of all other."

As I grow to understand life less and less,
I learn to love it more and more.

~ Jules Renard ~

Area 51

I wanted to include the lyrics to "Suicide" to help readers (hopefully) better understand, what I was going through during that darker time.

My prayer is that others feeling like I did will not express those feelings in violence and anger towards themselves or others, but find a more empowering and creative outlet. But most importantly, please know.... *you are not alone.*

Suicide

I sit here in the darkness
Just wondering where I've been
And as I think about my life
It's completely full of sin

I just don't have the friends
And my family sure doesn't care
So as I look around the room
I'm caught in a mental dare

Some people will say I'm crazy
To me it's all too real
No one out there to talk to
These walls know how I feel

(Pre-chorus)
I cannot deal with it anymore
My life is about to collide, with...

(Chorus)
Suicide, Suicide
Do it... Don't do it
Suicide, Suicide
Do it... Don't do it

I've got no faith or trust
This world is so demeaning
And with such a lack of confidence
Does my life have any real meaning

My head spins with the room
The anger continues to rise
Then I lay with a peaceful calm
And I finally come to realize

I cannot stop this thinking
And I'm not going to try
The last second gone from the clock
I'll leave with this Goodbye

(Pre-chorus)
I won't have to deal with it anymore
My soul is about to collide, with...

(Chorus)
Suicide, Suicide
Do it... Don't do it
Suicide, Suicide
Do it... Don't do it

Graphic Photos:

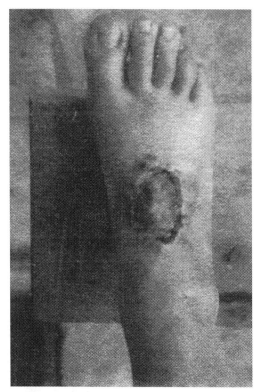

Dad's foot following surgery to remove the cancer.

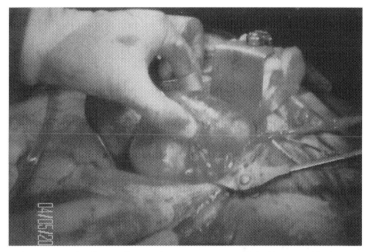

Rob's new kidney from his 22 year old deceased donor.

Kaley's brain surgery scar from reducing her cyst.

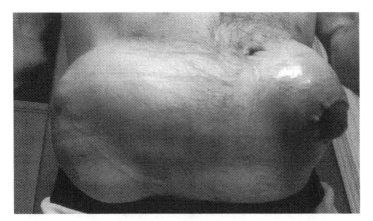

Rob's enormous hernias, fluid build up, and ostomy.

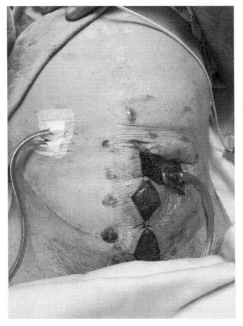

Incisions day of ostomy reversal surgery.

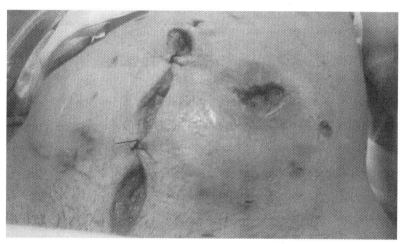

Incisions a few days after my ostomy reversal surgery

Printed in the United States
By Bookmasters